Union to Partition
Ireland 1800–1921

Russell Rees
Audrey M Hodge

Colourpoint
Educational

First Edition
Thirteenth Impression, 2011

ISBN: 978 1898392 07 1

Artwork: James Davis
Printed by: W&G Baird Ltd, Antrim

Cover illustration by Achille
Beltrane, from *La Domenica del
Corriere* (4 January 1920)

COLOURPOINT BOOKS
Colourpoint House
Jubilee Business Park
21 Jubilee Road
Newtownards
Co Down
BT23 4YH

Tel: (028) 9182 6339
Fax: (028) 9182 1900
E-mail: info@colourpoint.co.uk
Web site: www.colourpoint.co.uk

The authors

Dr Russell Rees and Audrey M Hodge MA are both
practising history teachers with many years' experience
of the Northern Ireland curriculum. They are co-
authors of *Ireland, Britain and Europe from 1570-1745*,
second edition published by Colourpoint in 1994; and of
Ireland and British Politics, 1870-1921 (Colourpoint in
1993).

Audrey Hodge obtained her MA in Modern and
Contemporary History at the University of Ulster. She
is the author of *Gallows and Turnkeys* which is a short
history of Omagh Gaol, *A Congregation in the Omey*
(1997) which is a history of First Omagh Presbyterian
Church, and *The Race to Rule* (Colourpoint 1998).

Dr Rees graduated in History with honours at the
University of Ulster and his doctoral thesis dealt with
the Northern Ireland problem between 1945 and 1951.
He is the author of *Ireland 1905–25 Vol 1: Text and
Historiography* (Colourpoint 1998) and *Nationalism and
Unionism in the Nineteenth Century* (Colourpoint 2001).

Acknowledgements

The authors and publisher would like to make the
following acknowledgements:

Mary Evans Picture Library: cover

Belfast City Council: 64A granted by kind permission of
Belfast City Council

National Museum of Ireland: 16A, 17C, 28A, 30A, 43B,
58B, 59C, 62A, 66A, 68A, 69C, 70B, 71F, 74B, 38A

Hulton Deutsch: 26B, 31C, 36B, 70A

Trustees of the Ulster Museum: 6A, 22C, 23F, 34A, 35D

Norman Johnston: 7B, 20A, 21F

Audrey Hodge: 50B, 51D

Dept of Agriculture for N. Ireland: 9B, 9C

Linenhall Library: 18A, 24A, 32A, 37C, 42A, 44A, 45A,
48A,B,C,D, 49E,F,G,H, 51C, 52B, 53D, 54B, 55C, 56A,C,
57D,E, 66B, 72A, 73D, 76B

Imperial War Museum, London: 63C

Milligan Estate: 38B

An Post: 40C, D, 41E, F

National Library of Ireland: 38C

Grateful acknowledgement is also made to Dr Margaret
Crawford of Queen's University, Belfast; Miss Christine
McIvor, Librarian, Ulster American Folk Park, Omagh;
Michael Kenny of the National Museum in Dublin;
and Dr Keith Jeffrey, of the University of Ulster
at Jordanstown, all of whom provided willing and
valuable assistance.

Contents

Part One: Ireland's Society and Economy

1.1	Ireland in 1800	4
1.2	Rural life before 1845	6
1.3	Causes of the Famine	8
1.4	The course of the Famine	10
1.5	Famine relief measures	12
1.6	Results of the Famine	14
1.7	Landlord and tenant	16
1.8	Solving the land problem	18
1.9	The Ulster linen industry	20
1.10	The growth of Belfast	22
1.11	Shipbuilding and links with Britain	24

Part Two : Attitudes to the Union

2.1	Unionism and Nationalism	26
2.2	Irish Republicanism	28
2.3	Repeal and Home Rule	30
2.4	Irish Unionism	32
2.5	Ulster Unionism	34
2.6	The rise of Parnell	36
2.7	Parnell and Kitty O'Shea	38
2.8	The Gaelic Revival	40
2.9	Killing Home Rule with Kindness	42

Part Three : Home Rule to Partition 1910 –1921

3.1	The Third Home Rule Bill 1912	44
3.2	Carson and Craig	46
3.3	Propaganda	48
3.4	The Ulster Covenant	50
3.5	The Ulster Volunteers	52
3.6	The Irish Volunteers	54
3.7	The Larne gun-running	56
3.8	The Howth gun-running	58
3.9	Ireland on the outbreak of war 1914	60
3.10	Irish Nationalists and the war	62
3.11	The Somme	64
3.12	The Easter Rising – origins	66
3.13	The Easter Rising – results	68
3.14	Markievicz – the Rebel Countess	70
3.15	The rise of Sinn Fein	72
3.16	The War of Independence	74
3.17	Partition	76
	Chronology	78
	Index	80

1.1   Ireland in 1800

The **Act of Union**, passed in 1800, joined Britain and Ireland together in the United Kingdom. Ireland no longer had its own parliament but was ruled by the Westminster parliament in London. For most ordinary people in Ireland this did not make much difference to their everyday lives for some time. Most people in Ireland were Roman Catholic but a large number of Protestants lived in north-east Ulster. This was partly because of earlier immigration from Scotland and England.

The population of Ireland in 1800 was approximately 4½–5 million. Only a tenth of these people lived in towns.

A

A single apartment ... rates from one to two shillings per week; and to lighten this rent, two, three, or even four, families become joint tenants ... ten to sixteen persons, of all ages and sexes, in a room of not fifteen feet square.

From Rev James Whitelaw's *Essay on the population of Dublin*, 1798

B

BELFAST population 20,000. The fifth largest city in Ireland and growing rapidly because of the booming textile industry. It had a police force and a good public water supply. Factory workers' houses were closely packed but they were too new to have become slums. The important men in Belfast were in the textile industries.

DUBLIN population 200,000. Even though there was no longer a parliament here, it was still a flourishing city, with very elegant Georgian buildings. A proper police force was set up in 1808. Some improvements were made for the poor, by building hospitals for them. It was a city of great poverty with many people living in slums and overcrowded tenements.

CORK population 80,000. A prosperous port, exporting mainly meat and butter. It had many rich merchants who were moving out of the city centre which sometimes got flooded. These people were living in fine new mansions in the valley of the River Lee. Cork also had many slum areas.

Use your library to find out more about the conditions in Belfast and Dublin at this time. From this information write a report called "The Condition of the Poor in Irish Cities".

Activity

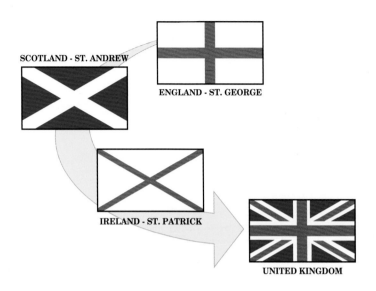

SCOTLAND - ST. ANDREW

ENGLAND - ST. GEORGE

IRELAND - ST. PATRICK

UNITED KINGDOM

This picture shows the different flags which come together to make up the Union Jack.

C

The Belfast Newsletter of 16th December 1806 estimated that the cotton industry in the town was employing 2,108 persons. In 1811 the Rev J Dubourdieu reckoned that these mills employed 22,000 (a wild over-estimate). In these years, cotton was king in Belfast: it was estimated that between 1800 and 1812 £350,000 was invested in cotton machinery there.

From *Belfast, an Illustrated History* by Jonathan Bardon

Government

The head of Irish government from 1800 was the Lord Lieutenant or Viceroy who was the King's representative. In Ireland he acted in the place of the King. He was assisted by the Chief Secretary who became more and more important and dealt with police, army and tax collection. He also went to the English parliament when Irish matters were being discussed. He was in charge of 22 civil service departments.

The counties were ruled by Grand Juries which were committees of local landlords. They looked after local issues such as road building and set the local tax rate.

In 1813 Sir Robert Peel, who was Chief Secretary in Ireland, set up a police force. They were nicknamed *Peelers* or *Bobbies*. By 1822 each county had some of this armed, trained and well paid police force.

1 What evidence is there in Source A that there was much overcrowding in Irish cities?

2 Using Source C, can we accurately describe Belfast as a 'cotton town' in 1800?

3 Why were the early policemen in Ireland nicknamed 'Peelers' or 'Bobbies'?

Questions

1.2   Rural life before 1845

A

This photograph was taken in Glenshesk, Co Antrim, probably around 1900. These girls are breaking up clods and smoothing the earth after the potatoes have been planted. Can you see the 'fairy thorns' which were never dug up, in case this brought bad luck?

Land ownership in Ireland in the early 19th century was in the hands of very few people. There were about 5 million people in Ireland. Only about 10,000 of these were landowners. These people were almost all Protestants. This system of only a few people owning land was a bit like the English system at that time. But in Ireland land was rented to tenants via a **middleman** and not directly from the landlord.

Types of farmer in Ireland

There were many classes of **tenant farmers** in Ireland. All of them paid rent to their landlord. Landlords often didn't live in Ireland at all, but lived on estates in England. These were called **absentee** landlords.

Strong farmers

These rented 30 acres or more and accounted for 5-10% of Irish tenant farmers. Their farms were often large grass farms on which they reared cattle for sale in Britain. Their homes were sturdy but not luxurious as most disliked spending their money on unnecessary things.

Small farmers

These rented farms between 5 and 30 acres. They formed the majority of Irish farmers. In Munster they were dairy farmers; in Leinster wheat was the main crop; in Ulster flax was widely grown. All of these farmers also practised mixed farming. Their houses were small and thatched.

Joint tenancies

These were families who joined together to rent a large piece of land. This system only existed in Ireland and was called **rundale**. Each family had a share of the arable and the pasture farming. People lived in a small village in poor houses. This system was beginning to disappear at the beginning of the 19th century.

Cottiers

These people rented less than 5 acres, usually ½ to 1½ acres, and formed the largest group in Ireland. They were mainly farm labourers who lived in miserable conditions.

There were two other types of labourer:

(a) young men and women hired at fairs, called **hiring fairs**, to live and work in the farmer's house

(b) **spalpeens** who wandered around the country looking for work wherever they could get it.

B

This is an example of a cottier's house. This house is at the Ulster Folk and Transport Museum at Cultra, outside Belfast. Can you see the "half door"? This is a door which is in two halves so that the top can be open and the bottom shut. Can you think of ways in which a door like this is useful?

A brighter side to life

Life for these farmers was not all poverty and hard work. There were many feast days, fairs and markets, such as Christmas and Easter as well as Shrove Tuesday and May Day.

Fairs in local towns were particularly popular. Everybody, from children to old people, went.

These fairs were crowded, colourful and noisy occasions providing a welcome change from the drudgery of daily life.

Markets were quieter and more businesslike. Most towns had a system of selling certain products on set days. Markets were important ways that the farmers got money. They sold their own local produce there.

A **tenant farmer** was a farmer who didn't own the land he farmed, but paid rent to the landlord who did own it. A **middleman** was a person who paid rent to the landlord and then sublet the land to tenants.

C

The young women carry their white stockings and dress shoes in their hands, going to the Cushendall Fair, till they are just at the entrance to the village; they then stop at the nearest stream and wash and dress.

Quoted in ME Collins, *Ireland Three*

Activity

Many travellers to Ireland in the 19th century described what they saw. Using the information in this unit, write a description of rural Ireland as if you were one of these travellers.

Questions

1 How did a spalpeen differ from a cottier?

2 What can we tell from Source C about the state of roads in the Cushendall area?

3 What was an absentee landlord?

1.3 Causes of the Famine

The population of Ireland increased very quickly in the first half of the 19th century. In 1841 a reliable census was taken and it estimated that the population of Ireland was then 8,175,000. In 1800 there were 5 million at the most.

We know that most of the people lived in the rural areas and depended on farming for a living. This rise in population meant more people needed land. Many farmers had **subdivided** their farms between their sons. When these sons eventually also subdivided land, the amount of land for each family was very small. In 1845, almost 200,000 families lived on less than 5 acres per family, while 135,000 families had less than 1 acre.

A

... in October 1845 came the first potato blight. We had a field of potatoes that year on the back lane and in one night they were struck with the blight and both tops and roots were blackened.

From the memories of
James Brown, a farmer from
Donaghmore, Co Tyrone

How subdivision worked

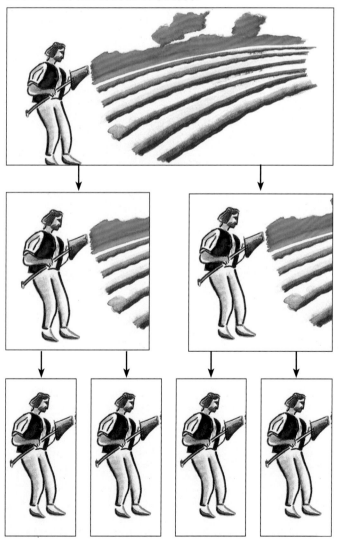

A farmer had 32 acres of land and four sons. He will divide his land between his sons. If each of these sons also had four sons, and so on, how many generations would it take for each son to be living on just half an acre?

A **census** is an official survey of all the people in a country to count them and to find out other useful information, such as how many people live in each house. To **subdivide** something means to divide it and then divide the divisions and then divide these divisions and so on.

This is what a blighted potato looks like.

A photograph of a potato plant which has been infected with potato blight. It is interesting that these photographs were taken by the Department of Agriculture recently. Potato blight is still a problem today.

It was only possible to live on such small plots of land because most of these people ate potatoes as the main part of their food. On average, a person ate 7lbs of potatoes per day and even quite a small plot of land could grow enough potatoes for most of the year.

For most families, however, there were at least two months of the year when the old potato crop was over and the new one was not ready. These were known as "hungry" or "meal" months when people were forced to eat a kind of porridge instead.

Famines were common in Ireland. There were fourteen partial or complete potato famines between 1816 and 1842 and one particularly bad one in 1740-41.

But in 1845 a new fungal disease struck the Irish potato crop. The big Latin name for it is *phytophthora infestans* — but it is usually just called **potato blight**! The first sign of a problem is when the leaves of the potato plant go black and die. By the time people noticed this, it was too late to save the potatoes, for the disease spreads especially quickly in moist, mild conditions. The potatoes became a stinking, soggy, black mess. Even if potatoes had apparently escaped this, the rot could still attack when they were stored in pits in the fields.

For the many Irish people who were almost totally dependent on the potato for food, such a blight caused disaster.

Questions

1 Explain how subdivision of land worked.

2 Why were the months when potatoes were in short supply sometimes called "meal" months?

3 What were the dangers of depending on potatoes for food so much?

4 How does Source A illustrate the speed of the blight?

5 Why do you think people in 1845 were not able to prevent this disease from spreading?

1.4 The course of the Famine

A

The little girl giving out clothes is seven years old, the daughter of Captain Kennedy, the Poor Law Inspector in Co Clare. He said "I was so maddened by the sights of hunger and misery ... that I [wanted] to take the gun from behind my door and shoot the first landlord I met."

Although one third of the potato crop was destroyed in 1845, the result at first was not a *shortage* of potatoes for eating, but far too many. Not all farmers had lost their crops. Those who hadn't, rushed to sell their potatoes before they went bad. However, by early 1846 supplies were exhausted and soon people were starving.

Sir Robert Peel was then Prime Minister and he decided to do something. He secretly bought £100,000 of Indian meal (maize) in America and had it brought to Ireland. Many people disliked the maize at first and called it "Peel's Brimstone". They were soon forced to eat it to prevent starvation.

The crop was not a total loss. But in 1846, when blight hit crops again, the failure was complete and this disaster struck a population already exhausted and starving. Fewer potatoes had been sown as many of the seed potatoes had been eaten. Death was widespread especially among the very poor in the west.

Fortunately the harvest of 1847 was a good one and, although the crop was smaller than usual, the situation was better that year.

However, the following year the blight struck again, but by 1850 the famine appeared to be over at last.

B

Indian corn and meal were introduced for the first time from America and I remember the poor people coming into the shop and asking to see "this yellow meal". They would then take some in their hand, ostensibly to look at it as a novelty, but really to satisfy their hunger with it.

From the memories of James Brown, a farmer from Donaghmore, Co Tyrone

C

Cowering wretches almost naked in the savage weather, prowling in turnip fields and endeavouring [trying] to grub up roots that had been left ... little children ... their limbs fleshless, their bodies half-naked, their faces bloated yet wrinkled and of a pale greenish hue [colour] – children who could never, oh it was too plain, grow up to be men and women.

John Mitchel describing the living

D

Oh I wish that we were geese, night and morn, night and morn;
Oh I wish that we were geese, night and morn.
Oh I wish that we were geese, then we all could be at peace,
Till the time of our release, eating corn, eating corn.

A verse from a labourer's famine song

E

There is a horrible silence ... We walk amidst the houses of the dead ... We stop before the threshold of our host of two years ago ... No answer. Ghastly silence and a mouldy stench as from the mouths of burial vaults. Ah! they are all dead.

John Mitchel, an Irish patriot, coming to a village in the west of Ireland

A **watershed** is a turning point.
An **ostensible** reason for doing something is not the real reason, but is meant to disguise the real reason.
A **novelty** is something new or unusual which makes you curious about it.

F

This picture tells another story from the Famine. This woman is Bridget O'Donnell. Her husband had 7 acres and the rent was about £7.25 a year. The family was evicted when they could not pay and men came to knock down their home. Bridget was pregnant and had a fever. Her husband went off to try to find work. Neighbours took in Bridget and her children. The baby was born dead and then they all got fever. Her 13 year old son died of hunger while the rest were sick.

The countryside and its people would never be the same again. Many regard the Great Famine as a watershed in Irish history and in Ireland's relations with the British government.

Many people died as a result of starvation but just as many died because of diseases which are associated with such starvation. These diseases, such as typhus and dysentery were very contagious and spread quickly in the overcrowded conditions.

The pictures of the famine on these two pages are of real people. They were drawn by an artist from *The Illustrated London News*. It was the first paper in the world to show the news in pictures.

The artist was sent to Ireland to cover the story of the Famine.

Activity

1 Make a simple time line of the years 1845–1849. Write down what happened to the potato crop each year.

2 Write a speech which a worried Irish MP might have made to the British House of Commons in 1847. He talks about what things are like in Ireland and asks the government to do something to help.

Questions

1 Do you think the pictures or the written sources in this unit are better at putting across the horrors of the famine? Explain your answer.

2 What evidence is there to suggest that the Irish were not very happy with Peel's purchase of maize?

3 What did Mitchel mean by the words in the last line of Source C?

1.5 Famine relief measures

Although the situation in Ireland was desperate the British government didn't usually interfere in matters to do with trade and the economy. This policy was known as **laissez-faire,** which is French for "let act". At this time the most important civil servant in the Treasury (where the British government's money was managed) was Charles Edward Trevelyan who was not sympathetic to the Irish. He thought of them as a disorderly race. He was more interested in saving money than in saving lives. But the government did take measures to help relieve the situation in Ireland.

A

Perhaps a road was started where a road was needed; the order would arrive that distress in that area was over and the work would stop ...

From *The Nation,* 29 August 1846

B

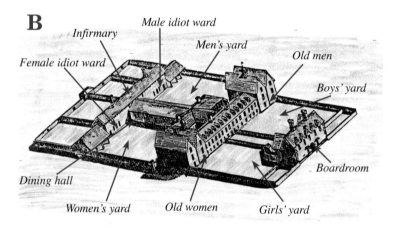

Male idiot ward
Infirmary
Men's yard
Old men
Female idiot ward
Boys' yard
Boardroom
Dining hall
Women's yard
Old women
Girls' yard

An Irish workhouse. Inmates were segregated into male and female, young and old. Even husbands and wives were separated.

C

The pay was 6d. and 7d. per day to the girls and women, and 8d. to the men, which was the lowest we met anywhere, though never exceeding 10d.

An English visitor describing the work scheme at Tobercurry, Co Sligo

D

At Tencurry and Turbid 3,200 quarts of porridge were distributed daily to upwards of 800 families, one of the boilers being filled four or five times. The amount of distress is greatly relieved.

Adapted from William Bennet's account, 1847

If you **emigrate,** you leave your own country and go to another country to spend the rest of your life there.

Activity

Divide into groups. Each group take one of the relief measures opposite and find out more about it. Report back to the whole class what you have discovered. Discuss which of the relief measures you think was the best one. Is there one which you do not think was a good idea?

Workhouses

People avoided workhouses as much as they could until the famine left them no choice. By January 1847, there were 111,000 people in workhouses built to accommodate 100,000. This overcrowding just added to the problems of disease spreading and 'famine fever' became widespread. More people died of these diseases than of hunger.

None of these measures was enough to end the hardship. Added to this were the many diseases which accompanied the famine. So many died and were buried in mass graves that nobody is sure exactly how many died. Diseases like oedema, scurvy and typhus were common and little could be done to prevent them.

Many people decided the only other thing to do was to flee Ireland and emigrate to Britain or America. Huge numbers of people emigrated but many did not live to see the new land and died on the journey to America. Even those who survived were not sure of a warm welcome.

Soup kitchens

After stopping the work schemes, Trevelyan suggested a new plan - the local ratepayers would provide soup kitchens to feed the starving. The landlords did not wish to encourage the use of these soup kitchens because they had to pay for them, so they made them as unattractive as possible. The food was nasty and poor and was always ready cooked so people could not sell the raw ingredients. Anyone with more than a quarter of an acre of land did not qualify for food.

The "soup" was a type of porridge called "stirabout" and each person was to get one pound per day.

In general, these soup kitchens worked well.

Public works

These were schemes which were partly funded by local rates (taxes) and provided some very basic work for the needy so that they could be paid and then buy food, instead of receiving charity. The hours of work were very long. The pay was poor and very uncertain.

Even though pay was often late many people were so desperate that they would hang around a work scheme waiting for a worker to collapse so that they could get his job. In October 1846 there were 114,000 on works like these. By February 1847, there were 700,000. Trevelyan said this was costing too much and by June 1847 nearly all work had ceased.

Private charity

This came from various sources. Irishmen in the Indian army sent £50,000. A private committee in Dublin collected £63,000. Queen Victoria sent £2,000. Many landlords lost much money in trying to help; others did almost nothing. The Society of Friends (Quakers) gave food, clothing and seeds where they were most needed. This group was also useful for sending back to England accurate reports of the Irish situation. Many in America, especially those of Irish origin, did much to send help to Ireland.

1.6 Results of the Famine

A

To **decline** in number means to get less and less.

This picture shows the deck of an emigration ship. Only the wealthier emigrants were allowed to use the deck. Poorer people often had to stay below for the whole voyage, which could be three months. Disease thrived in these conditions and many died on the ship.

Population decline

One of the most obvious effects of the famine years was the decline in the population of Ireland. In 1851 the population was down by almost 2 million from the previous census (1841). Half of this number had died; the rest emigrated. Not only was there this immediate effect on the population, but the population continued to decline and in 1900 was only about 4½ million. Much of this was due to the changing pattern of early marriage and land subdivision.

B

This vessel left with 476 passengers, of whom 158 died before arrival, including the Master, mate and nine of the crew ... Three days after her arrival there remained of the ship's company only the second mate, one seaman and a boy, able to do duty; all others were dead or ill in hospital.

Quoted in *The Potato Famine and the Irish Emigrants* by PF Speed, 1976

Consolidation of land

Many landlords were anxious to sell off their land, especially if they were in debt. The Encumbered Estates Act of 1849 made it easier for them to do so. Many tenants had realised the uncertain nature of subdivision of land and had stopped doing it. The number of larger holdings increased and the cottier class almost died out.

C

Land holdings in 1841 and 1851

Acres	1841	1851
1 - 5	310,436	88,083
5 - 15	252,799	191,854
15 - 30	79,342	141,311
over 30	48,625	149,090

Abstract from the census returns of 1841 and 1851

Change in marriage patterns

This change in land distribution had important effects on society. Now, in order to keep the farm as one unit, only one son could inherit and he had to wait until his father died before this could happen. This often led to later marriage and a subsequent decline in birth rate.

It also meant that other sons and daughters often saw emigration as the best solution for their future.

Political effects

Many in Ireland resented the actions taken by the government or at best saw them as inadequate. This helped to make the Irish even more bitter towards England. Such bitterness took root in the new emigrant communities in England and especially in America.

Emigration

This was widespread following the famine years as many tried to find a new life in a better land. However, many never reached the new land but died in the awful conditions on board what were often called **coffin ships**. These ships were overcrowded, food was poor and disease spread rapidly. All of these made worse their feelings of bitterness towards Britain.

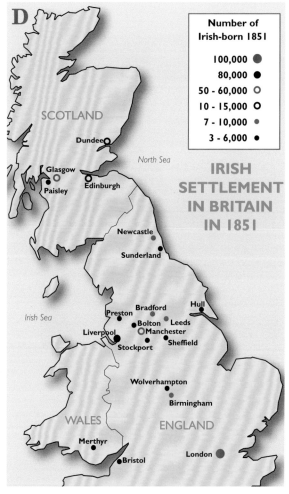

This map shows some towns in Britain, in 1851, which had many people who had been born in Ireland living in them.

In August 1849, Queen Victoria visited Ireland and was welcomed with popular enthusiasm. However this was not an indication that the relations between the two countries were at all good at this time. The Famine left a feeling of bitterness.

Activity

Write an article explaining how the social and economic conditions in Ireland are different in 1851 from those in 1841.

Questions

1 What does Source C tell us about the changing size of Irish farms?

2 Look at Source D – which were the four towns with the largest Irish-born population?

3 Can you think of reasons why these four towns attracted so many Irish immigrants?

1.7 Landlord and tenant

This picture shows a Land League banner from Kilmally, Co Clare. The side above shows Michael Davitt and carries the slogan "Down with Landlordism". The other side of the banner shows Parnell.

After the Famine the prices of many agricultural products, such as meat and butter, rose rapidly. This made Irish farmers richer but this prosperity didn't last long for many. It gave landlords the perfect excuse to raise the rents which their tenants paid. However after 1876, prices began to fall again and many tenant farmers fell on hard times. Their situation was worsened (in the years 1877-79) by very bad weather which ruined many crops. In many parts of Ireland, especially the very poor areas of the west, famine seemed likely again. Added to these problems was the fact that the landlords were still insisting upon getting their rents. Tenant farmers were evicted or driven off their land if they could not pay. In an effort to protect themselves from evictions the farmers joined together in a new movement. The man who led them was **Michael Davitt**, the son of an evicted tenant farmer from Co Mayo.

The Land League

Davitt wanted to get support from **Charles Stewart Parnell** who was leader of the new Home Rule movement. So in June 1879, Parnell was invited to speak at a protest meeting of tenant farmers in Westport, Co Mayo. At the meeting, Parnell was given huge cheers when he called on the tenant farmers to stand together and fight evictions. Later in 1879 the **Land League** was formed and Parnell became its first President. The new movement had several aims: it wanted to reduce rents, stop evictions, and help tenant farmers become owners of their farms.

Parnell and Davitt knew they needed each other for most Irishmen were more interested in the land question than in Home Rule. Through the Land League the Home Rule Party was put in close touch with the tenant farmers, and this link between Home Rule and the land question became known as the **New Departure**.

B

Now what must we do in order to induce [persuade] the landlords to see the position? You must show them that you intend to hold a firm grip of your homesteads and lands ... You must help yourselves, and the public opinion of the world will stand by you and support you in your struggle to defend your homesteads.

From a speech by Parnell at Westport, Co Mayo, 8 June 1879

C

This shows a family being evicted from their home.

D

... Captain Boycott, the manager of Lord Erne's estates in Co Mayo. Local people refused to work for him in Lord Erne's house or on his land. Labourers were brought in from Ulster, protected by hundreds of police and troops, but life became so unbearable for Boycott that he had to leave. From then on the word 'boycott' was used for this sort of action. In this case Lord Erne reduced all rents by a tenth so the boycott was successful.

From *Modern Ireland* by EG Power, 1988

The Land War

In their fight with the landlords the Land League used a new tactic called the **boycott**. If a family was evicted, anybody who moved into the farm would be treated as an outcast or **boycotted** by all his neighbours. If this failed to drive him away, the new farmer could have his house attacked at night. In fact between 1879 and 1882 the violence was so bad that it became known as the **Land War**.

The British Prime Minister who had to try to deal with this unrest was the Liberal leader, **William Ewart Gladstone**.

The aims of the Land League

1 To organise tenant farmers to help themselves.
2 To reduce rents.
3 To stop evictions.
4 To help tenant farmers to become owners of their farms.

Activity

Construct a timeline showing the main events in the history of the land question. Use these dates to help you:

	1876
	1877 - 79
June	1879
Autumn	1879
	1879 - 1882

Questions

1 Why did it seem a good idea to involve Parnell in the land question?

2 What evidence is there in Source A to show that Parnell and the Land League were working for *all* of Ireland?

3 Would a tenant farmer listening to Parnell's speech (Source B) have felt (a) encouraged or (b) worried by the things he said?

4 Read Source D. What effect did the boycotting seem to have on Lord Erne? Explain your answer.

1.8 Solving the land problem

A

THE RIVALS.

This is a cartoon from the English magazine *Punch*, 13 August 1881. Look at it carefully. There is a question about it.

B

[The Act of 1881] seemed to give the Ulster tenants all that they had asked for; they received it with jubilation [great joy]; and they made immediate use of the new procedure for adjusting rents. It is symptomatic [a sign] of their attitude that at a by-election in Tyrone in 1881 a Land League candidate was defeated by a Liberal.

From *The Making of Modern Ireland* by JC Beckett

C

Landlords and tenants alike were dissatisfied with the Acts of 1891 and 1896 ... But both sides hoped for better terms and in 1902 they combined to bring pressure on the government.

From *The Making of Modern Ireland* by JC Beckett

Land ownership

The English government was very alarmed by the Land War and in an effort to stop the violence, it passed the **1881 Land Act**. This set up special land courts to decide what was a **fair rent**. Once this was settled, a tenant who paid this rent could not be evicted. This reduced rents by an average of 20%. However, nothing was done for the poorest farmers who still could not pay their rents. As a result the violence in the Irish countryside continued.

A **grievance** is something about which you feel unhappy and complain. Something is **inefficient** if it does not do very well what it is meant to do.

In 1886 the Conservatives formed a new government. They believed that the Irish did have some real grievances about land ownership so they decided to do something about this. In 1891 and 1896 two Acts were passed which suggested very complicated ways of lending money to tenants for land purchase. These did not work well and agitation continued.

In 1902 a **Land Conference** was arranged at which landlords and tenants met to work out a scheme which pleased both sides. This led to the **Wyndham Land Act** of **1903**. This Act gave £100 million to help tenants buy their farms. To encourage landlords to sell, they were given a bonus of 12% if they agreed to sell their entire estate at once. Tenants who got loans under the terms of this Act were to repay them over 68½ years. This Act was very successful and between 1903 and 1920 about eleven million acres of land changed hands. Ireland was no longer a land of tenant farmers but of landowners.

D

The success of Wyndham's Act was immediate. At the time of its passage there were still more than half a million tenant farmers. By 1909 some 270,000 purchases had been made, and a further 46,000 were pending [waiting]. Little more than a decade later, landlordism in rural Ireland had become a thing of the past.

From *The Making of Modern Ireland* by JC Beckett

Activity

1 List the stages in land purchase in Ireland in chronological order.

2 Write a short article encouraging farmers to join a 'co-op'.

Questions

1 Identify the rivals in the cartoon, Source A.

2 What methods are they using to win over Ireland?

3 Using the information in this unit, explain which method had most success.

4 Why do you think the Land League candidate in Tyrone did not win the 1881 by-election? (Source B)

5 What was unusual about landlords and tenants combining to put pressure on the government? (Source C)

Improving conditions and methods

Irish farmers were not very prosperous even though they owned their land. Prices for agricultural produce were low and farming methods were backward and inefficient. In 1899 the government set up the **Department of Agriculture** to try to teach better farming techniques.

The head of this department was **Sir Horace Plunkett** who came originally from Co Meath. He suggested to farmers that they should form co-operative groups to sell their goods and buy essentials like fertiliser in bulk. He formed the **Irish Agricultural Organisation Society** in 1894. At first many people were rather suspicious of this idea but by 1914 there were over a thousand "Co-ops" throughout Ireland. It was an idea particularly popular among dairy farmers.

The Ballyduggan weaver's cottage. This is a cottage which has been reconstructed at the Ulster Folk and Transport Museum at Cultra, Co Down. The loom occupies all of the part to the left of the front door. The family lived in the rooms to the right.

The linen trade spread all over Ulster in the 18th century and was always closely associated with farming. The weavers were farmers who took on this extra job to add to their living from the land. The flax was often grown locally and spun into yarn by the women of the household. Many of these families had a full size loom in one room of their cottage. Most of the fabric was sold at markets or sold back to merchants who had supplied the yarn for weaving. Such work, done in the home, was known as the **domestic** or **cottage system** of industry.

The reeling room inside Ewart's linen mill, Belfast, about 1890. The yarn is being wound onto large revolving frames.

B

Shipbuilding was male, mostly Protestant, and a symbol of the union or 'Britishness'. Linen was much more mixed.

From *Belfast – Portraits of a City* by Robert Johnstone, 1990

D

Linen and ships made Belfast utterly different from any other place in Ireland, and perhaps helped alter the political fate of the whole island.

From *Belfast – Portraits of a City* by Robert Johnstone, 1990

Many linen market towns grew up in Ulster and especially in the Lagan Valley. **Belfast** was one such town. It had a Linen Hall and trade increased throughout the 18th century. By the turn of the century the **cotton industry** had moved to Belfast and did much to turn the small town into a city. Belfast production of cotton could not compete with the Lancashire mills and it declined in Ulster, because, after 1820, English cotton could be imported into Ireland without any duty (tax) on it.

Dunbar and McMaster's linen mill, Gilford, Co Down

G

Numbers employed in the Irish linen industry

1871	55,000
1875	56,000
1885	62,000
1896	69,000

Questions

1 In what ways did the linen industry help to make North East Ulster different from the rest of Ireland?

2 Study the pictures of the weaver's cottage (Source A) and of the large mills (Sources C and F). How would life and work in one of these large mills have been different from the domestic system of industry?

E

It needs but a glance at Belfast and its surrounding country to perceive that the town and its neighbouring districts have nothing in common with the rest of Ireland.

From *Ireland in 1834: a journey throughout Ireland* by HD Inglis

Activity

There were at least 15 stages in turning the flax plant into linen cloth:

pulling, rippling, retting, gaiting, breaking, scutching, roughing, combing, hackling, drawing, spinning, reeling, weaving, bleaching, beetling.

Either on your own or in groups, see how many of them you can find out about.

Factories

However, the cotton industry had brought textile factories to Belfast and many people had moved to work in the mills. The scene was now set for linen manufacturing to move from the home to the Belfast factories. The North-East of Ulster saw the growth of huge factories with tall chimneys dominating the landscape and the noise of giant steam engines filling the air.

Case Study 1.10 The growth of Belfast

Belfast was by far the most important industrial city in Ireland. To every visitor it looked just the same as the other new industrial towns in Britain such as Liverpool, Manchester and Glasgow. It clearly was not like any other *Irish* town or city. As its industry grew, Belfast's population rose quickly. In 1800 it was less than 20,000, but during the 19th century Belfast became the fastest growing city in the British Isles. By 1850 its population was over 100,000 and by 1900 it was nearly 400,000. Industry was booming and large numbers came to the city looking for jobs in the linen mills.

The workers who moved to the city were both Protestant and Catholic, but rather than live together the two groups felt safer if each lived in its own area. As a result Belfast had its Protestant working class districts and its Catholic working class districts. In fact, many of these districts remain today. This division of people into separate areas is known as **segregation**.

Segregation was needed because from time to time trouble would break out between the two communities. Fighting like this was described as **sectarian violence**. As the city grew, sectarian riots became more and more common, and they were particularly bad in 1857, 1864 and 1872. The point to note here is that sectarian violence was common in Belfast long before the political problems caused by the first Home Rule Bill in 1886.

A

Belfast's population of 20,000 at the time of the Union had expanded more than ten times that number by the late 1880s ...The population of Dublin in the same period only doubled. At the same time Belfast ... became one of the most thriving industrial cities of the United Kingdom.

From *The Bold Fenian Men* by Robert Kee, 1972

B

In Belfast they had large steel and iron ship-building yards where fathers and sons could be employed. They also had ... the linen industry, where the wives and daughters found employment. If there was not sufficient employment in these places, they had the largest rope manufacturing establishment in the world.

Speech by James Henderson, Lord Mayor of Belfast, to the Irish Trades Union Congress in 1898

C

The launching, in May 1911, of the *Titanic* which was built at Harland and Wolff's shipyard in Belfast. Note the lack of the four distinctive funnels – at the time of the launch the *Titanic* was still incomplete and the funnels, along with much of the upper-deck work and the interior, would be added later. Eleven months later, on 15 April 1912, the *Titanic* sank on her maiden [first] voyage. About 1,500 people died.

Belfast's industry

As well as the linen industry, Belfast began to develop a number of other industries, which also paid well and employed many workers. One of these industries was engineering. To begin with, they made linen machines, but by 1900 they were making the steam engines, water turbines and all the other parts needed for new ships. The **shipbuilding industry** also helped to encourage the city's **ropeworks**, which by the end of the 19th century was the largest ropeworks in the world.

E

Number of Roman Catholics
working for Harland and Wolff in:

1864	225
1887	77

Many names still associated with Belfast today originated in this period of industrial growth in the 19th century.

James Mackie, a Scot, was manager of a factory making textile machinery when it went bankrupt and he took it over.

Edward Harland set up the Belfast Ropework Company in 1873; **Gustav Wolff** was its Chairman.

The **Sirocco** works became world leaders in ventilation and fan manufacture by the end of the century as a result of Samuel Davidson setting up his own tea-drying machinery works in 1881.

Thomas Gallaher moved his tobacco firm from Derry to Belfast in 1863. By 1902 he was also making cigarettes. Gallaher's was the largest tobacco factory in the world.

William Dunville and **James Craig (Senior)** built a large modern whiskey distillery on the Grosvenor Road in 1870.

John Boyd Dunlop came to Belfast from Scotland in 1867 to practise as a veterinary surgeon. In 1887 he made the first working pneumatic tyre for his son's bicycle.

D

Religious problems in the work force [at Harland and Wolff] recurred [happened again] ... In 1872 during the tension surrounding the Home Rule debates, which led to rioting in the town, 500 men left work early and fought a battle with police ... Catholics were being forced out of their homes in Protestant areas ... from which the Harland and Wolff workforce was largely drawn.

From *Shipbuilders to the World (Harland and Wolff)* by M Moss and JR Hume

John Dunlop riding a bicycle with pneumatic tyres

Questions

1 Why did so many people move into Belfast in the 19th century?

2 What evidence is there in this unit of sectarian trouble?

Activity

1 The four main industries in Belfast were linen, shipbuilding, rope making, and tobacco. Design a poster about Belfast in the late 19th century showing all these.

2 Write a newspaper article for the Belfast Newsletter in January 1901 giving an account of the progress the city had made in the last hundred years.

1.11 Shipbuilding and links with Britain

A

ULSTER'S PRAYER
Don't let go!

A postcard printed around the end of the 19th century, supporting the union with Britain

Cork had been the shipbuilding centre of Ireland in the first half of the 19th century. Belfast had few resources vital for this industry. However, the Harbour Commissioners did much to make the Lough suitable.

In 1858 Robert Hickson sold his yard to his manager Edward **Harland** who received much of the money he needed to buy it from G. C. Schwabe of Liverpool and his nephew Gustav **Wolff**.

In 1870 the firm signed a contract with the **White Star Line** and this marks the beginning of the yard's success. Its first White Star ship was the **Oceanic**, the first modern liner.

The success of Harland and Wolff continued throughout the 1890s, overshadowing the smaller firms such as Workman Clark & Company.

The development of industries helped to make many in North-East Ulster even more determined to maintain their links with Britain.

Belfast was also a very important port. It brought in the coal needed by the new steam engines of the Industrial Revolution. Coal was vital for industry and as there was hardly any coal in Ireland it had to be brought from Britain.

B

By 1886 the Ulster Protestant felt joined to the United Kingdom by something much more strong than just their opposition to a Catholic Ireland. Their whole way of life and industry was completely bound up with the U.K.'s prosperity. As a result, any plans to separate them from Britain were seen as plans to ruin their prosperity.

Adapted from *The Bold Fenian Men* by Robert Kee, 1972

Look carefully at Source A. With a partner, try to explain why each area has been given the name written on it.

Activity

Britain was also the main market for the new goods made in Ulster. Linen cloth was sold to Britain and to many parts of the British Empire. The ships made by Harland and Wolff were sent to the Royal Navy and to the great British shipping companies like the White Star Line.

So for Belfast and North-East Ulster the economic link with Britain was vital. Earlier, it was the province's large number of Protestants which made Ulster, especially North-East Ulster, different from the rest of Ireland. Now industry could be added to the list, because while farming was still important throughout Ireland, it was only around the Belfast area that industry had developed quickly. As this industry grew, North-East Ulster became more and more closely linked to the industrial areas in Britain. Belfast was certainly much more like Glasgow and Manchester than it was like Dublin.

C

The industrial revolution in the North East ... separated Ulster from the rest of Ireland, for the North East relied mainly on Britain and abroad for markets and raw materials ... The result was that Ulster hardly ever looked southwards and had more in common with Merseyside and Clydeside than the rest of Ireland.

From *A History of Northern Ireland* by Patrick Buckland, 1981

D

To our mind, the progress of Ireland since the Union, and especially since the famine, affords the strongest ... proof that her future should be even more prosperous than her past ... Why should we fear the future now, when we are so much better prepared to meet it?

From *The Union Vindicated. Ireland's progress 1782–1800–1886*, a pamphlet published by the Irish Loyal and Patriotic Union, 1886

Titanic

This is probably the best known ship built by Harland and Wolff but it was not regarded as extra special at first. It was launched on 31 May 1911 and Harland and Wolff had not even bothered to paint the hull white for the launch. The ship, when completed, left for Southampton on 3 April 1912 and was mentioned briefly in the local Belfast Newsletter.

"At eleven o'clock this morning she [*Titanic*] will leave Belfast for Southampton ... the decorations and equipment are on a scale of unprecedented magnificence and it is difficult to realise when standing in some of the spacious saloons or staterooms that one is really on board a ship and not in a large modern hotel. Special interest was manifested in the suite of rooms for millionaires and other wealthy passengers ...".

On 10 April the ship left Southampton, calling at Cherbourg and Queenstown and on to the Atlantic. At 11.40 pm on 14 April she struck a huge iceberg and at 2.20 am on 15 April she sank. Only 711 of 2201 passengers survived.

It was the journal *The Shipbuilder*, not Harland and Wolff, which claimed the *Titanic* was "virtually unsinkable".

If something is **vital**, it is absolutely necessary and cannot be done without.

1 What does Source A tell us about the fears of many Ulstermen?

2 Look at Source C. Why was North-East Ulster so dependent on Britain and abroad?

3 Can you think of other evidence which an historian would need to have, to give him the full picture of the fears of Ulstermen at this time?

Questions

2.1 Unionism and Nationalism

In 1798 up to 50,000 Irishmen took part in a rebellion to try to set up an Irish Republic free from British rule. The rebellion was poorly organised and was easily put down, but it shocked the British government.

It was clear that a new way of governing Ireland had to be found, and in 1801 the **Act of Union** came into force. This Act got rid of the Irish parliament in Dublin, which had been there for 500 years. From 1801 Ireland was part of the United Kingdom and was governed from Westminster. The Irish were entitled to send 100 MPs to the London parliament at Westminster.

A

To our mind the progress of Ireland since the union ... [provides] proof that her future should be even more prosperous than her past ... why should we fear the future now ...?

From a Unionist pamphlet, 1886

B

A picture of a debate going on inside the House of Commons at Westminster in London in 1852. At the back, wearing a long wig, you can see the **Speaker** who referees the debates.

At the front, on the table, the long pole with the crown at one end, is called the **mace**. This represents royal authority, and debates can only take place when it is there.

Look at television pictures of debates in the House of Commons today and see if you can see any of these things still there.

Obviously, the Act of Union gave the British full control over Ireland. Many Irishmen were against this. Upper-class Protestant landowners were immediately affected by the new union. They were the people who had held seats in the Irish parliament, so they were unhappy because they had lost power. But soon they came to see the benefits of the union.

Later in the 19th century these upper-class Protestants became the leaders of **Irish Unionism**, which was a new movement dedicated to maintaining the union between Britain and Ireland. Nearly all of those who supported the union were Protestants.

Study the key elements in nationalism on the opposite page. Take each in turn and discuss whether this element united or divided the Irish people at this time, and how it did so. For example – language: most spoke English but some spoke Irish.

26

But even more people in Ireland were against the union. These anti-unionists were later called Nationalists. Unlike Unionism, nationalism was a powerful force in many other parts of Europe in the 19th century. Then, much of Europe was ruled over by great empires which were often made up of many different groups of people.

A good example was the Austrian Empire which had eleven different national groups. As the 19th century went on and nationalism became a stronger force, these different groups wanted to break away from Austria and form their own countries. Many in Ireland wanted to do the same. The boxes on the right can help us understand nationalism.

C

It has been hinted to us that it is our opinion that no-one but a Catholic can be an Irishman. We never said so, nor do we think so.

From *The Leader*, a Nationalist paper, in 1901

While Irish nationalism contained some of these key elements, others were missing. For example, although the Irish had their own language, only a very small number of people actually spoke Irish.

Another problem was religion. Most Irish Nationalists, though not all, were Catholics, but as we have seen, Ireland also contained a large number of Protestants.

So, in the 1800s, there were two new political forces in Ireland, both brought about by the union:

1 The Unionists who wanted to keep the union with Britain.
2 The Nationalists who wanted Ireland to be independent.

Key elements in nationalism

Geography
Some countries stand out on a map because they have natural borders such as rivers or mountains. Islands are the best example of this.

Race
Nations will often contain people from the same race. The main feature separating the different races is the colour of their skin.

Language
If each nation or country has its own language, it helps to bind its people together and show that they are different from others.

Culture
People who share the same culture, which includes literature, music, games and customs, will feel a common bond.

Religion
Sometimes religion can be a common factor which binds a group or nation together.

Questions

1 According to Source A, what is the main reason put forward by the Unionists for keeping the union with Britain?

2 Study Source C. Why do you think some people had said that only a Catholic could be an Irishman?

2.2　Irish Republicanism

Wolfe Tone and the United Irishmen

The rebellion in 1798 had been a hopeless failure, but it was a very important event in the history of Irish Nationalism. The men who took part in the rebellion admired the American colonists who had fought the British and won independence in the early 1780s.

Then in 1789 the French Revolution broke out. This gave a lot of new political ideas to Irishmen who wanted their country to be independent from Britain. In 1791 they formed the **Society of United Irishmen.** One of their new leaders was **Wolfe Tone** who was a Protestant lawyer from Dublin. Most of the other leaders of the United Irishmen were Belfast Presbyterians.

Tone and the other Protestant leaders of the United Irishmen believed that they would only win if most of the people in the country supported them. In Ireland most of the people were Catholic. The aim of the United Irishmen was to use force to set up an independent Irish Republic. This established the republican tradition in Irish Nationalism.

Above:
This is a membership card for the 1798 Memorial Association, issued in 1898.
The flag on the left is the French tricolour which came into use after the French Revolution in 1789.
The flag on the right shows the dawn of Irish Nationalism.
The cap in the centre represents 'liberty' and was worn by the revolutionaries in France.
On the top leaf of the shamrock is written 'Ireland'; on the left leaf 'Ulster' and 'Munster' and on the right leaf 'Connaught' and 'Leinster'.
A pair of hands is clasped in the centre. The pictures around the card show scenes connected with the United Irishmen. The one on the bottom left shows Robert Emmet's rebellion of 1803.

Robert Emmet

After the 1798 rebellion failed, Wolfe Tone committed suicide in prison while waiting to be hanged. But despite their failure, the United Irishmen had set an example that future Irish Republicans looked back to.

The next try at revolution was in 1803 when **Robert Emmet** led a rebellion in Dublin. It turned out to be a disaster and Emmet was executed. Now Irish Republicans had two new martyrs to follow – Tone and Emmet.

B

Let the man among you who has no gun, sell his garment and buy one.

Written by the Young Irelander, John Mitchel

Questions

1 Which important events in the story of Irish Republicanism took place on the following dates — 1791, 1798, 1803, 1842, 1848, 1858, 1867?

2 What did John Mitchel mean by the words quoted in Source B?

The Young Irelanders

In 1848 there was yet another rebellion. This time it was organised by a group called **Young Ireland**. Ever since 1842 the Young Irelanders had been writing about their ideas in a weekly newspaper called The Nation, which printed lots of articles about the differences between England and Ireland.

As we saw in Unit 1.4, Ireland in 1848 was suffering from the effects of the famine, and the people had no interest in a revolution. Only about 100 people took part in the Young Ireland rebellion and it was easily crushed. Go back to pages 8 to 15 to remind yourself about the Famine.

The Fenians

The Famine was so bad that the country took years to get over it, but in 1858 a new group with the old aim of using force to win Irish freedom was set up. This was the **Fenian** movement. To begin with it looked as if the Fenian movement might be more successful, because it was supported by thousands of Irishmen who had emigrated to America. But when they staged their rising in 1867, it was just another one on the list of republican failures.

The Fenian movement was also known as the **Irish Republican Brotherhood (IRB)**, and though the 1867 rising had been defeated, the IRB continued to operate secretly, planning for another rebellion. In this way it kept alive the republican tradition. Yet republicanism had changed from the days of Wolfe Tone and the United Irishmen. With each rebellion Irish Republicans widened existing divisions in Ireland between Protestants and Catholics.

A **martyr** is someone who dies for the cause that they believe in.

Activity

1 Find out what was meant by the symbols referring to France in Source A.

2 Talk about possible reasons why the Irish republicans of 1798 should have used these symbols.

2.3   Repeal and Home Rule

Daniel O'Connell

Not very many people in Ireland supported republicanism, which used violence. Far more people preferred a peaceful, moderate approach and wanted to persuade the British to make improvements in Ireland. The Act of Union allowed the Irish to send 100 MPs to Westminster, but all of these MPs had to be Protestants even though eighty per cent of the people in Ireland were Catholics. In 1829 this was changed when **Catholic Emancipation** was granted. This allowed Catholic MPs to sit in parliament. A man called **Daniel O'Connell** had led the campaign for Catholic Emancipation. He was a wealthy Catholic lawyer.

After this success O'Connell began a new campaign to repeal (remove) the Act of Union and bring back an Irish parliament. Soon he was addressing huge outdoor meetings all over the country. To help organise this campaign O'Connell worked closely with the Catholic Church.

Even though O'Connell had the backing of most Irish Catholics, the British government wouldn't give in and refused to repeal the Act of Union. O'Connell believed in using peaceful methods. He could see that if he went on, violence could break out. So he stopped his campaign for repeal, including cancelling a monster protest meeting planned for Clontarf in 1843.

A

Daniel O'Connell, known as "The Liberator" because of his work for Catholic Emancipation

B

I would not ... fling the British connection to the winds ...

From a speech by Daniel O'Connell in Parliament, 1834

Isaac Butt

Although O'Connell had failed, he had got people to see that peaceful ways could work. This way was more popular with Irishmen than the violence of the Irish republicans. When the Fenian rising of 1867 failed, many Irishmen thought that it was the right time to go back to the peaceful methods of constitutional nationalism. Their leader was **Isaac Butt**. He formed the **Home Rule League**.

In 1874 there was a general election and the Home Rulers won 59 seats. This new Home Rule Party wanted a separate parliament in Dublin. This did not mean that Ireland would have complete freedom or independence from Britain. The new parliament would only look after local affairs, such as education and road building, leaving the Westminster parliament in overall control. Therefore, Home Rule was a moderate aim which fell somewhere between the union and independence.

Gladstone

Of course, if Home Rule was to be successful, it would have to be passed by the parliament at Westminster. At that time, the two great parties at Westminster were the **Liberals** and the **Conservatives**. The Irish MPs knew that they had to win over one of these two great parties. Here the Irish Nationalists were in luck because the Liberal leader, **William Ewart Gladstone**, wanted to make changes in Ireland. In one of his famous early speeches he had said: "My mission is to pacify Ireland", which made the Irish think that he could be persuaded to back Home Rule. They were right. Gladstone introduced the first Home Rule Bill in 1886. Parliament did not pass it but Gladstone was not put off. He introduced a second Home Rule Bill in 1893. It was defeated too, but many Irish Nationalists thought that at last they were getting somewhere. They hoped that it would only be a matter of time before a Home Rule parliament was sitting in Dublin.

C

William Ewart Gladstone in 1877. His hobby was cutting down trees!

D

We can claim the privilege of managing our own affairs by a parliament ... in Ireland.

E

There should be in Ireland an administration for Irish affairs, controlled by the Irish parliament.

From *Proceedings of the Home Rule Conference*, held in Dublin, 1873

Getting a Bill passed in Parliament

Before an Act has been passed by Parliament it is called a Bill. There are two Houses in Parliament – the House of Commons and the House of Lords. A Bill is usually debated by the Commons first, but even if they agree to it (that is, *pass* it) it then has to go to the Lords who must agree to it too before it can become law.

Questions

1 When O'Connell cancelled the Clontarf meeting, the words "God Save the Queen" appeared at the bottom of the notice. Using Source B, suggest reasons why he would have used this slogan.

2 How would an Irish Republican have viewed O'Connell's views about the British connection?

3 How was Home Rule different from Republicanism? Looking back at Unit 2.2 might help you with this question.

2.4　Irish Unionism

Loyal Ireland

does not require or want Home Rule in any shape. We implore the people of Great Britain to use their influence to overthrow the forces that would terrorize and ruin the industrious, and drive the country to desolation.

From ....

Printed and Published by John Cleland & Son, Ltd., 68 & 70 Gt. Victoria St., Belfast.

A

Postcards like these were signed and then posted to friends in Great Britain.

Remember how, in unit 2.1, we saw that those who wanted to keep the union between Britain and Ireland were called Unionists. Most of these Unionists lived in North-East Ulster. In the 1885 general election the Unionists won 18 seats, nearly all of them in Ulster, and all of their MPs voted against the first Home Rule Bill in 1886.

There were Unionists outside Ulster. In the rest of Ireland about 10% of people were Unionists. They were just as determined to fight Home Rule as the Unionists in Ulster. Because there were so few of them, these Southern Unionists didn't often fight elections against the Irish Nationalists. Instead they tried to get people in Britain to stand against Home Rule. They held meetings all over England and sent out thousands of leaflets to persuade as many British voters as possible to support the union.

B

Since March [1892] three million leaflets dealing with [Home Rule] have been scattered ... throughout England, Ireland, Scotland and Wales. At present, the committee is engaged distributing 250,000 pamphlets in support of the union throughout the various polling districts of Lancashire.

From a report of Irish Unionists, 1893

The Irish Unionist Alliance

In 1891 these Unionists formed the **Irish Unionist Alliance** to fight Home Rule. Although small in numbers, the Irish Unionist Alliance was a powerful group, because many Southern Unionists gave a lot of money to support the campaign against Home Rule. In fact, a lot of Southern Unionists were very rich. Many were big landowners, while others were wealthy businessmen from Dublin and Cork.

Two of their best known leaders were Lord Lansdowne and Lord Midleton. They actually owned big estates in England as well as Ireland. Lansdowne, Midleton and about 80 other leading Southern Unionists were members of the House of Lords in London and they used their influence to put the case against Home Rule. This gave the Southern Unionists very close links to the Conservative party in England.

Conservatives

Earlier, we saw how Liberals in Britain helped Irish Nationalists to try to win Home Rule. On the other side Irish Unionists, especially Southern Unionists, got help from the Conservative party in their struggle against Home Rule. The Conservative party was known as the party of empire. At the time Conservatives were afraid that if Ireland was given Home Rule, other countries in the British Empire would want to be treated the same. They thought this could lead to the break-up of the Empire itself.

This explains why they gave their full support to Irish Unionists in the fight against Home Rule. In fact, during this period the Conservatives were often called British Unionists. This was a good description.

Irish Unionists and British Unionists also believed that Home Rule would be the first step on the road to complete independence for Ireland. They could not believe that the Nationalists would settle for a Home Rule parliament and not full independence.

C

Conservatives and Unionists in Britain and Ireland feared that any concessions would spark off a chain reaction and lead to the eventual break up of the British Empire.

Adapted from *A History of Northern Ireland*, by Patrick Buckland, 1981

Questions

1 What evidence is there in this unit that Irish Unionists directed much of their attention to Great Britain?

2 Why do you think they did this?

3 Explain how Irish Unionists could use the Empire question to their advantage in England.

4 What was the main disadvantage of having two Unionist groups in Ireland?

Southern Unionists and Ulster Unionists

Although both the Southern Unionists and the Ulster Unionists were equally determined to defeat Home Rule, there were many differences between them. The main difference was that Ulster Unionism was much more anti-Catholic than Southern Unionism. In the South the Unionists needed the local Catholics who worked as farm labourers and servants on the big estates. As there were so few of them, Southern Unionists could never think of using force to defeat Home Rule. Of course, this did not apply in the North-East where there were far more Unionists. Also, Southern Unionists were nearly all drawn from the wealthy classes, while in Ulster, Unionist supporters included big landowners, rich businessmen, and also small farmers and poor workers. These differences were to grow during the next few years.

Differences between Ulster Unionists and Southern Unionists

Ulster	Southern
Were more anti-Catholic	Depended on their Catholic countrymen who worked for them on their big estates
Were both rich and poor	Were nearly all rich
Because there were so many of them they could use force if they wanted to	Too few of them to be able to use force

2.5 Ulster Unionism

A photograph taken of the Ulster Unionist Convention of 1892, held in the Botanic Gardens, Belfast. *Erin go bragh* means "Ireland for ever".

When the time came to fight Home Rule, most people expected Unionists in Ulster to lead the way. As we have seen, the fact that they formed a majority in North-East Ulster meant that, unlike the Southern Unionists, they did not need to look elsewhere for support. Ulster Unionists could rely on themselves to defeat Home Rule. They were able to use the Orange Order to organise resistance to Home Rule. The Orange Order had been formed in 1795 to defend Protestant interests. They did not work as closely with the Conservatives in Britain as the Southern Unionists did, but they were happy to get Conservative support when it came.

When Gladstone, who was a Liberal, decided to go for Home Rule in 1886, the Conservatives took the chance to make a split in the Liberal Party by coming out strongly against Home Rule. This was the attitude of the leading Conservative, Lord Randolph Churchill, who visited Belfast in February 1886. Here he told Unionist supporters that they could always count on the support of British Unionists. Later, he encouraged the Ulstermen to use force when he said **"Ulster will fight and Ulster will be right"**.

The prospect of Home Rule really worried the Ulster Unionists. Look at the box on this page to see why. The worries caused by the first Home Rule Bill also led to a new wave of sectarian fights in Belfast. In the summer of 1886 nearly 50 people were killed in rioting between Protestant and Catholic workers.

B

I decided some time ago that if [Gladstone] went for Home Rule, the Orange card was the one to play.

Lord Randolph Churchill, February 1886

Why the idea of Home rule worried the Ulster Unionists

1 They felt their Protestant religion would be threatened.

2 If the link with Britain was broken the new linen and shipbuilding industries would not have enough money to survive.

The Second Home Rule Bill 1893

Although the first Home Rule Bill had been defeated, Unionists knew that the next Liberal government might bring in a new bill. In order to show how much they were against it, Ulster Unionists organised an Ulster Unionist Convention which met in Belfast in June 1892. It was held in the Botanic Gardens where a giant wooden pavilion was built. About 12,000 attended. About one-third of these Unionist supporters were ordinary tenant farmers who had come from all over Ulster, but it was clear that their leaders were from the upper and middle classes. They sat on a special platform which held 400 people. Many of these 400 people were either big landowners or rich businessmen. The Convention Chairman was the Duke of Abercorn who owned a big estate in Co Tyrone.

During the Convention many of the speakers warned that Ulster Unionists would never accept Home Rule. Some of them even said that violence could be used if Home Rule was forced on them. Yet in spite of these threats, Gladstone, who was back again as Prime Minister, introduced the second Home Rule Bill in 1893. This time the bill was passed in the House of Commons, but it was easily defeated in the House of Lords, where there were a lot more Conservatives. If Home Rule was ever to become law, it would have to be passed by both houses of parliament. In Unit 3.1 we will see a way round this problem.

C

One with Great Britain, heart and soul
One life, one flag, one fleet, one throne.

These words of a British poet appeared above the platform at the Ulster Unionist Convention in 1892.

Remember!

Conservatives supported the Unionists. Most of the Liberals supported Home Rule.

D

This is a painting of a riot in Belfast in the nineteenth century. Notice how different the buildings looked then. The scene is possibly at the lower end of Sandy Row, since the Boyne Bridge is in the background.

Activity

1 Think of all the reasons why the Ulster Unionists and British Conservatives wanted to keep the union. Using these reasons, design a pro-union poster which might have been used at the time.

2 Write a short newspaper report or caption that might have been printed with the picture of rioting in Belfast – Source D.

Questions

1 Why would the banner outside the Convention Hall in 1892 have had on it the Irish words meaning "Ireland for ever"?

2 Explain what you think is meant by the four items mentioned in the second line of Source C.

2.6 The Rise of Parnell

Although Isaac Butt (see page 30) deserves credit for organising the new Home Rule party, he did not turn out to be a very good politician. Even before he died in 1879 one of his fellow Home Rulers, **Charles Stewart Parnell**, had more or less taken over from him as leader of the party. Parnell had only become an MP in 1875, but in his first speech in parliament he showed that he was a strong Nationalist when he warned other MPs "Ireland is not a geographical fragment. She is a nation".

Isaac Butt had behaved like a gentleman but Parnell was tougher in parliament. To force MPs from the other parties to pay attention to Ireland's problems, Parnell, along with a handful of other Home Rulers, held up business in parliament by speaking for hours at a time. They talked so long that MPs often had to sit right through the night. This tactic was known as **parliamentary obstruction**, and it was very successful. Because of it, a lot more people heard about the Home Rule cause.

A

If you refuse to pay unjust rents; if you refuse to take farms from which others have been evicted, the land question must be settled, and settled in a way that will be satisfying to you. It depends, therefore, upon yourselves ...

From Parnell's speech to tenant farmers in Ennis, Co Clare, in 1880

Charles Stewart Parnell

He was a Protestant.
He was a landowner.
He was educated in England.
He spoke with an upper class English accent.

This picture of Parnell appeared in the magazine *Vanity Fair* in 1880.

Parnell's background made him very different to his fellow Home Rulers. Look at the box above to see how he was different.

But these differences helped to make him an outstanding leader. With Parnell in charge it was certain that the campaign for Home Rule, both in Britain and Ireland, would get stronger. In order to win more support for Home Rule in Ireland Parnell knew that he would have to win over the country's huge number of tenant farmers. When he was invited to speak to a protest meeting of tenant farmers in Co Mayo in 1879, Parnell jumped at the chance.

Later that year the Land League was formed and Parnell became its first President. The link between the Land League and the Home Rule movement was known as the **New Departure**. By asking the government to introduce land reforms, Parnell was sure to get the support of the tenant farmers in his fight for Home Rule.

As we saw in unit 1.7, the violence from 1879-82 was known as the **Land War**. Parnell was even jailed for six months for his role in it. When he was released in 1882, Parnell played down the land question and began to concentrate on Home Rule.

The 1885 general election was a great success for the Home Rule Party. It won 86 seats. This made it clear to Gladstone that most people in Ireland were keen to have Home Rule and in April 1886 he introduced the first Home Rule Bill. Under Parnell's leadership the Home Rule Party had become a united and well organised group in parliament. As he really wanted to have their support, this must have influenced Gladstone when he decided to introduce Home Rule.

Although the Liberals had won 333 seats in the 1885 election, both Gladstone and Parnell knew that many of these would not be persuaded to support Home Rule. When the vote came, 93 Liberals voted against it, and the first Home Rule Bill was defeated by 343 votes to 313. Following the bill's defeat Gladstone resigned as Prime Minister, but Parnell was not too unhappy. It had been a great achievement to have a Home Rule Bill brought before parliament, and they had persuaded Gladstone to support Home Rule.

The Home Rulers knew that when the Liberals next won a general election, they could still get Home Rule.

C

STRANGLING THE MONSTER.

This cartoon appeared in the humorous magazine, *Punch*, 5 February 1881. Who is the monster and who is strangling him? Notice the reference to Obstruction.

D

I have often thought that Parnell was like Napoleon. He allowed nothing to stand in his way. He stopped at nothing to gain his end ... He was indifferent [didn't care] about the means he used to gain his object.

From Joseph Chamberlain's description of Parnell

Questions

1 In what ways was Parnell different from most Home Rulers?

2 Why was it important to Parnell to get the support of tenant farmers?

3 If you were a tenant farmer listening to Parnell's speech (Source A) would you have felt hopeful that the land question would be satisfactorily answered? Explain your answer.

4 Using the information in this unit, say how Parnell would have been viewed by (a) a supporter and (b) an opponent at this time.

2.7   Parnell and Kitty O'Shea

Captain William O'Shea

Parnell, drawn from life
two months before he
died in October 1891

Katharine O'Shea

At the time of the first Home Rule Bill Parnell was the most popular leader that Irish Nationalism ever had, but something was about to happen which would cause his downfall.

While in England, Parnell had been involved in a love affair with Katharine (Kitty) O'Shea, the wife of another Home Rule MP. The Irish leader had first met Kitty in 1880 and they soon became lovers. In fact, they lived together in England and had three children. Many Irish MPs knew about it, but it was only when Kitty's husband, William O'Shea, named Parnell as his wife's lover in a divorce case that everybody heard about it.

Many of Parnell's supporters in Ireland were shocked. There the Catholic Church was very unhappy with Parnell's behaviour, and it wanted him removed as leader. This was serious because most Home Rule supporters in Ireland were Catholic, and it was difficult to see how Parnell could continue as leader when the Catholic Church, which was very powerful, was against him. Gladstone also made it clear that if Parnell remained as leader, he would drop his support for Home Rule.

Activity

Using the information in this unit and the last one, write a short report or obituary about Charles Stewart Parnell.

D

...his [Parnell's] continuance at the present moment in the leadership would be disastrous for the Irish cause and would mean that I could no longer remain leader of the Liberal Party.

Adapted from a letter by Gladstone, 24 November 1890

The Parnellite split

Surprisingly Parnell thought that he could beat this opposition and stay on as leader. Things came to a head in Committee Room 15 in the House of Commons in December 1890 when the Home Rule MPs voted about their leader. Bitter clashes took place between those for and those against Parnell. When the votes were counted only 32 had supported Parnell with 54 voting against him. The party which Parnell had made into such a powerful force had dropped him as leader. Those who had supported him were called the **Parnellites**. Those against him were known as the **anti-Parnellites**.

Despite his defeat Parnell would not give up without a fight. He returned to Ireland and toured the country making speech after speech. Here there were three by-elections coming up, and Parnell believed that the by-elections would give him the chance to show that the people still supported him. But by this stage Parnell was being fiercely attacked by the Catholic bishops. The three by-elections were in North Kilkenny, North Sligo and Carlow. In all three places, Parnell's candidate was easily beaten by an anti-Parnellite.

A **by-election** is an election held to fill a vacancy when there is *not* a general election taking place. An MP might have died or resigned and a new MP has to be elected to fill his place until the next general election. An **obituary** is a short life story of someone who has just died.

Questions

1 Why did the divorce scandal affect Parnell's political career so much?

2 Study Source E. Is the writer hopeful that a new leader will be found who is as good as Parnell? Explain your answer.

Parnell's death

Still, Parnell would not give up, but his travels all over Ireland had left him very ill and he died in England in October 1891. He had married Kitty in June 1891, but the two had little time to spend together. When he died, he was only 45. His funeral was held in Dublin, and was attended by huge crowds. Irish Nationalism had lost its best leader, and the Home Rule Party was now divided.

E

Remember our Chief! – (who can guide us no more) –
He rests on his laurels, his troubles are o'er;
He's gone that long journey where all ends in peace,
Where all controversy and politics cease.
Ah! had we but one to put in his place,
And not leave our country in sorry disgrace!
We can't find his equal, alas! we know well;
Our chieftain is gone, Charles Stewart Parnell.

From a ballad by Edward Mayfield, Dublin 1891

2.8   The Gaelic Revival

While most Irishmen were happy with the work of the Irish MPs at Westminster, others did not like waiting for Home Rule to be passed. After all, this would only be done when the Liberals were ready to try again. While the Home Rule leaders were waiting for this to happen, those unhappy at the delay turned to different ways of showing their nationalism. One thing was clear; they were Irish, not English, and they wanted to show this. So even before 1900 a new movement had appeared which helped to spread fresh ideas about Irish Nationalism.

The Gaelic Athletic Association

This began in 1884 when the Gaelic Athletic Association (GAA) was formed in Co Tipperary. It organised the playing of Irish games such as hurling and Gaelic football to replace English games such as cricket, rugby and tennis. Soon the GAA had 50,000 members, and it was very strong in rural areas. At Parnell's funeral GAA members, carrying their hurleys like rifles, formed a guard of honour.

A

The League shall be strictly non-political and non-sectarian.

Item 8 of the Gaelic League constitution

B

When we look out on Ireland we see that those who believe ... in Ireland a nation are, in fact, Catholics ...

From the newspaper which supported the Gaelic League, July 1901

C

D

These two stamps were issued by An Post (the Post Office of the Republic of Ireland) to mark the centenary of the Gaelic Athletic Association. The one above, 22p value, pictures hurlers from Cork (red) and Kilkenny (stripes). The other one, 26p value, shows footballers from Kerry (green and gold) and Dublin (blue).

E

F

These two stamps were issued by An Post in 1993 to celebrate the centenary of the Gaelic League. They show different aspects of Irish culture.

The Gaelic League

Yet even more important than the GAA was the Gaelic League. It was founded in 1893 by **Douglas Hyde**, the son of a Protestant minister from Co Roscommon, and **Eoin MacNeill** who grew up in Glenarm, Co Antrim.

Hyde and MacNeill wanted Irish people to use the Irish language or Gaelic as it was known. It had almost died out and was spoken only in the poorer areas in the far west of the country.

The Gaelic League soon attracted new members who could see that reading and speaking Irish was the best way to show that they were different from the English.

This type of nationalism was known as **cultural nationalism**. Unlike the GAA, the Gaelic League was stronger in towns where its language classes were very popular with younger, well educated people.

Activity

The leaders of the Gaelic Revival felt that learning Irish and playing Gaelic games was very important. In groups, discuss why they thought so and whether you agree with them.

Questions

1   Which English sports do hurling and Gaelic football resemble?

2   One founder of the Gaelic League was a Protestant from the province of Connaught.
The other was a Catholic from Ulster. What does this tell you about the founders of this movement?

3   Does Source B suggest that the Gaelic League (Source A) was successful in being non sectarian?

4   Why do you think this was?

5   Which aspects of Irish culture are shown in Source E?

2.9 Killing Home Rule with Kindness

PAT (in the tall hat): "What d'ye think of the Home Rule Bill, Murphy?"
MURPHY: (puzzled): "Begorra, if it means staying at home with the ould woman every blessed day, Home Rule won't do for me at all!"
A cartoon in the London magazine *Punch*, April, 1893

When Gladstone resigned after the defeat of the first Home Rule Bill in 1886, the Conservatives took over. However, all the fuss over Home Rule had forced the Conservatives to take a fresh look at Ireland. They believed that the land question was the real root of the problem in Ireland.

In the late 1880s there was a big fall in the prices farmers got for their produce. This meant that farmers had less money and many found it hard to pay their rents. Landlords began to throw farmers and their families out of their homes if they couldn't pay. This was called eviction (see Unit 1.7). There were more and more evictions. The farmers took new action to force landlords to lower their rents. This new **Plan of Campaign**, as it was called, was led by **John Dillon** and **William O'Brien**.

To deal with the Plan of Campaign the government sent **Arthur Balfour** to Ireland. He wanted the Irish to forget about Home Rule and to do this he tried a new policy. Those breaking the law in the countryside were to be severely punished. But Balfour also saw that something had to be done to sort out the land question. He believed that a new set of measures, which would give better treatment to the farmers, could show the Irish that the English government was fair and so they would have no need for Home Rule. This new policy was known as **Killing Home Rule with Kindness**.

B

I am for ... repression as stern as Cromwell; reform as thorough as Mr. Parnell can desire.

Balfour speaking when he was sent to Ireland in 1887

Land purchase

The Conservative government wanted to help the Irish tenant farmers to become owners of their own land. But the farmers were poor so for this to happen the government would have to lend money to these tenants so that they could buy their farms from the landlords. A start on this had been made in 1885, but, as we saw in Unit 1.8, it was the **1903 Wyndham Act** which really changed the pattern of land ownership in Ireland. The Act said that £100 million was to be given for buying land. In a short time Ireland was changed from a country of tenant farmers into a country where the farmers, not the landlords, owned the land they farmed. This policy of Killing Home Rule with Kindness was used over twenty years from 1885 to 1905.

C

Arthur Griffith

D

(1) Ireland to have a parliament of her own in Dublin.
(2) The King of England to remain as King of Ireland.
(3) An Irish parliament to run the country without English interference.
(4 The British government in Ireland would be ignored wither away.
(5) If Ireland was to be really independent, she also had to be economically independent; to buy Irish goods and place taxes on foreign goods.

The aims of Sinn Fein when it was founded in 1905. Note the second one. In 1905, Arthur Griffith still supported the monarchy.

Activity

Design a recruiting poster for the new organisation, Sinn Fein, in 1908. (It was not called Sinn Fein until this date.)

Questions

1 Study Source A carefully. Is this a reliable source for the Irish farmers' understanding of the Home Rule question?

2 How does Source B show the two sides of Balfour's approach to Ireland?

Sinn Fein

In spite of the success of land purchase, many people still wanted Home Rule. In fact, during this period a growing number of people began to think that a simple Home Rule parliament in Dublin would never be enough for Ireland. One such man was **Arthur Griffith**. In 1905 he set up a new group later called Sinn Fein. In his weekly newspaper, *United Irishman*, Griffith argued that Ireland should have more independence. Still, while many people knew of Sinn Fein's views, most Irish people continued to support the Home Rule party. At the beginning of the 20th century an older group of hard-line republicans was also beginning to reorganise. This was the IRB. Shortly after 1900 the IRB began to attract younger, more determined members who might one day take part in a new rebellion against Britain.

3.1 The Third Home Rule Bill 1912

A

NO THOROUGHFARE !

A postcard from the period

B

I said earlier it is impossible to grant Home Rule. The opposition of Ulster ... makes it impossible ... I was present last week at a gathering of the [Ulster Unionists at Belfast] ... It was the expression of the soul of a people. They say they will not submit, except by force, to such a government.

Speech in the House of Commons by Bonar Law, 16 April 1912

The constitutional crisis

There was a general election in 1906. The Liberals were voted back into government. They got such a huge majority that they did not need the Home Rule Party's support. By this stage the Home Rule Party was often known as the **Irish Parliamentary Party (IPP)**. Its leader was **John Redmond**. He had reunited the party after the Parnell split. Redmond knew that Home Rule was not going to happen soon. So he planned to wait patiently until the Liberals needed the support of the Home Rulers. This came sooner than expected.

In 1909, the House of Lords, where there were a lot more Conservatives than Liberals, refused to pass the budget, because it included a new tax on the rich. This defeat of the budget raised the question of which of the two Houses of Parliament – the House of Commons or the House of Lords – should have more power. The Liberal Prime Minister was **Herbert Asquith**. He insisted that the House of Commons should have more power because the people elected the MPs there.

There was so much debate about it that Asquith called a general election in 1910 to try to solve things. This didn't work because the two main parties finished very close together, and a second general election was held later that same year. This time the Liberals won 272 seats, exactly the same as the Conservatives, while the IPP (the Home Rulers) won 84 and Labour 42. So now the Liberals needed Redmond's support, because the IPP held the balance of power.

House of Lords

The members of the House of Lords are not elected by anybody. They are members because they were born with a title, like Lord Salisbury, or because of their job. For example, the Archbishop of Canterbury is a member of the House of Lords just because he is an Archbishop.

The Parliament Act 1911

The controversy over the House of Lords was known as the constitutional crisis, but now there was a chance for a simple deal to solve this problem. If the Irish MPs would support a new bill to reduce the powers of the House of Lords, Asquith (the Liberal Prime Minister) could introduce a third Home Rule Bill.

Of course, this suited the IPP because the House of Lords would have to be changed in some way if Home Rule was ever to become law. So Redmond was happy to support the new law. So when the **Parliament Act** was passed in **1911**, it said that the House of Lords could no longer throw out a bill but only hold it up it for two years. After this it would become law.

C

Carson: "Take it away, it smells; been buried twice already; bury it again, this time *for good*."

1 With a partner, study the two cartoons (Sources A and C). Decide what is meant by each character, label and comment.

2 Suggest how cartoons like this could be useful to an historian of these events.

3 Apart from cartoons and Source B, what other types of sources would you need to build a fuller picture of events in 1912?

Questions

The Third Home Rule Bill 1912

Now the Irish Nationalists had a way of getting round the House of Lords. It seemed that the IPP could actually get Home Rule for Ireland.

Asquith introduced the third Home Rule Bill in April 1912. He was not as strong a believer in Home Rule as Gladstone had been. In fact, if he had not needed Redmond's support after 1910, Asquith would probably have steered clear of Home Rule altogether. This meant that the link between the Liberals and the Irish Nationalists was not as strong as it appeared, and yet just at this time the link between the Conservatives and the Unionists was becoming stronger.

The reason for this was the new leader of the Conservative Party, Andrew Bonar Law. When he took over in 1911, Bonar Law found that the Conservative Party was divided and weak. To unite the party Bonar Law decided that he should make opposition to Home Rule his priority. This was not surprising because Bonar Law's father had lived in Ulster, and he himself had very close links with the province. Indeed he was the one leading British politician who had a good understanding of the reasons for Unionist opposition to Home Rule.

So as long as Bonar Law remained leader, Ulster Unionists could count on the full support of the Conservative party in their fight against Home Rule.

3.2 Carson and Craig

Sir Edward Carson

Sir James Craig

When the new Home Rule Bill (the third) was discussed in parliament, nearly every Unionist speaker raised the question of Ulster. They claimed that there were two different sets of people in Ireland. Not only were there two religions, there were two races or even two nations in the country.

For the Unionists it followed that if Ireland was to be given Home Rule, then Ulster should also receive special treatment. Yet for these Unionists the aim was not to win special treatment for Ulster, but to use Ulster opposition to force the Liberal government to drop Home Rule altogether.

C

We must be prepared ... the morning Home Rule passes, ourselves to become responsible for the government of the Protestant province of Ulster ... Our motto is "We rely on ourselves".

From Carson's speech at Craigavon, September 1911

Activity

Use your school library and reference books to find out more about Carson and Craig. Write a short life story of each of them.

Carson

The best speaker on the Unionist side was **Sir Edward Carson**. He set out to use Ulster to block Home Rule. Carson had become Unionist leader in 1910. In one way Carson was a strange choice to lead the Ulstermen, because he was a Southern Unionist from Dublin and his home was in London. However, Carson was a brilliant public speaker and a very clever leader.

The first chance most Ulster Unionists got to hear Carson was in September 1911 when he spoke to 50,000 Orangemen gathered at Craigavon, **Sir James Craig's** home just outside Belfast.

D

Sir James Craig's private home at Craigavon, Co Down

Craig

Sir James Craig was a perfect deputy for Carson. Craig was quiet, solid and reliable, and he was a terrific organiser. He used his talents to organise a number of mass protest meetings, like the one held at Craigavon. Although the two men had very different personalities, together they formed a very powerful leadership team which was to direct Ulster Unionist resistance to Home Rule through the very difficult times which lay ahead.

E

I said to Churchill that you would appoint your own police and allow no other body to interfere with your action.

From a letter sent to Edward Carson by Bonar Law, 18 September 1913

Protest meetings

Another huge protest meeting was held at Balmoral, which is near Belfast, in April 1912, just two days before Asquith introduced the third Home Rule Bill. A crowd of 100,000 turned out to listen to the Unionist speakers who included Bonar Law, the new Conservative leader. Later in July 1912 Bonar Law spoke to a Unionist gathering in England. He warned the Liberal government that there were "things stronger than parliamentary majorities". By this he meant that even if Ulster Unionists used force to resist Home Rule, the Conservative party would stand behind them.

So by the summer of 1912 it was clear that if the Liberals pushed ahead with their Home Rule Bill, violence could break out in Ulster.

Questions

1 What impressions do the photographs give you of Carson and Craig?

2 Describe the sort of house which Craig owned.

3 What evidence is there in Sources C and E that the Ulster Unionists were serious in their rejection of Home Rule for Ulster?

3.3 Propaganda

Using Source E as a guide, with a partner think of a familiar landmark in your home town and produce a Unionist card showing your town under Home Rule.

Activity

This was produced as a stamp rather than a postcard (shown twice actual size).

E

BELFAST UNDER HOME RULE. Making a site for the statue of King John the First of Ireland. It says: "Tickets for New York or anywhere".

·HOME·RULE· F

·AN· ORANGEMAN·IN·ULSTER·

In the struggle over Home Rule both Unionists and Nationalists tried to put forward their own points of view and win support for their very different aims. Remember that there was no television or radio at this time. So to influence people they used **propaganda**. This propaganda included posters, newspaper advertisements, labels, pamphlets and postcards. All of these ways could spread ideas. If a political message could be passed on in a cartoon, it was often even more popular, so leaders of both parties liked to use cartoons.

G IRELAND A NATION

HOME RULE HEROES

Behind this Statesman Leader, true and grand,
You'll find that faithful, patriotic band
Of heroes, who have lived to make our land.

A NATION

A postcard with a picture of John Redmond

ULSTER'S SOLEMN COVENANT H

SIR EDWARD CARSON.

HEROES OF THE UNION

Behind this gallant Statesman are men who lead the cause,
The glorious cause of Union. Men of Ulster! do not pause.
We have signed the Solemn Covenant, which binds us to defend
Our faith, our flag, our loyalty unflinching to the end.

A postcard with a picture of Sir Edward Carson

Questions

1 Sort the postcards on these two pages into three sorts:

- Unionist;
- Nationalist;
- unclear which side.

2 Compare the pictures of Redmond and Carson (Sources G and H). List the ways in which they are similar.

3 These two pictures were produced by the same firm. What does this tell us about this firm?

3.4   The Ulster Covenant

The huge protest meetings in Ulster had shown that resistance to Home Rule didn't have to be only in parliament, but could happen in other places too. More and more people were joining the Orange Order, and as the summer of 1912 approached, feelings were running high between the two communities in Belfast. It was no surprise when a new wave of sectarian rioting broke out in the city.

The violence worried the Unionist leaders who knew that their fight against Home Rule would not be successful unless they could control their followers better. What their campaign needed was something which could give Ulster Protestants a focus and also win further support for the Unionists' point of view in Britain.

A

After religious services in the churches, when the hymn "O God our help in ages past" was sung, a procession headed by Carson and the faded yellow silk banner, said to have been William III's at the Battle of the Boyne, marched through the streets to Belfast Town Hall, escorted by a guard of honour of 2,500 men in bowler hats, carrying walking sticks.

Adapted from *The Bold Fenian Men* by Robert Kee, 1972

B

Ulster's
Solemn League and Covenant.

Being convinced in our consciences that Home Rule would be disastrous to the material well-being of Ulster as well as of the whole of Ireland, subversive of our civil and religious freedom, destructive of our citizenship and perilous to the unity of the Empire, we, whose names are underwritten, men of Ulster, loyal subjects of His Gracious Majesty King George V., humbly relying on the God whom our fathers in days of stress and trial confidently trusted, do hereby pledge ourselves in solemn Covenant throughout this our time of threatened calamity to stand by one another in defending for ourselves and our children our cherished position of equal citizenship in the United Kingdom and in using all means which may be found necessary to defeat the present conspiracy to set up a Home Rule Parliament in Ireland. ¶ And in the event of such a Parliament being forced upon us we further solemnly and mutually pledge ourselves to refuse to recognise its authority. ¶ In sure confidence that God will defend the right we hereto subscribe our names. ¶ And further, we individually declare that we have not already signed this Covenant.

The above was signed by me at _Mountjoy_
"Ulster Day." Saturday, 28th September, 1912.

David McFarland

─── God Save the King. ───

Ulster Day

28 September 1912

Craig hit on the idea of a **Solemn League and Covenant** for Ulster. This turned out to be a brilliant idea. The plan was that as many citizens as possible would sign a copy of the Covenant during a week of organised meetings in September 1912, when leading Unionists from England and Ireland would tour Ulster. The week was to end with a huge demonstration in Belfast on Saturday 28 September. This was called **Ulster Day**.

Left: The Covenant signed by Unionist men

Right: The Covenant opposite was the version signed by Unionist women.

Carson himself signed the Covenant in Belfast's City Hall with a silver pen presented especially for the occasion. He was followed by the rest of the Unionist leaders. All over Ulster ordinary people signed the Covenant, and to show how strongly they felt some even signed in their own blood! When the figures were added up, over 450,000 men and women had signed the Covenant.

Ulster Day: Sir Edward Carson signing the Covenant, Belfast City Hall, 28 September 1912

D

Ulster's
Solemn League and Covenant.

Text of the Covenant made by the Ulster Women's Unionist Council, and which has been signed by the loyal women of Ulster in token of their unwavering hostility to Home Rule:—

WE, whose names are underwritten, women of Ulster, and loyal subjects of our gracious King, being firmly persuaded that Home Rule would be disastrous to our country, desire to associate ourselves with the men of Ulster in their uncompromising opposition to the Home Rule Bill now before Parliament, whereby it is proposed to drive Ulster out of her cherished place in the Constitution of the United Kingdom and to place her under the domination and control of a Parliament in Ireland.

Praying that from this calamity God will save Ireland, we hereto subscribe our names.

The above was signed by me at O mugh
"Ulster Day," Saturday, 28th September, 1912.

God Save the King.

The day was considered a great success. English newspapers told their readers of the great discipline and determination shown by Ulster Unionists during this special week of activity. So the Ulster Covenant not only allowed the Unionist leadership to win back full control of their followers, but it also meant that they got some very good publicity in England.

Questions

1 What three things did Unionist men, who signed the Covenant, agree to? (Source B)

2 What were the women agreeing to do? (Source D)

3 Suggest reasons why there were two versions of the Covenant.

3.5 The Ulster Volunteers

We have seen that, in 1912, there was a lot of talk about giving special treatment to Ulster. But what was Ulster? Not everybody was talking about the same thing. The Ulster Covenant that you read about in the last unit, talked about the *province* of Ulster, which had *nine* counties. (It still has today.) But in June 1912 when MPs were discussing possible ways to satisfy Unionist objections to Home Rule, one suggestion was that an area of four counties could be left out of the Home Rule scheme. These were the four counties in North-East Ulster, Antrim, Down, Londonderry and Armagh, where the Unionists had a very big majority.

From a JP's Certificate

The reason behind this idea was that Unionists in Ulster were threatening to use force if they were placed under a new Home Rule parliament in Dublin. Of course, any talk of special treatment for even four counties of Ulster made Redmond and his fellow Irish Nationalists angry. They made sure that Asquith (the Prime Minister) and his Liberal government stuck to their plan of introducing Home Rule for the whole of Ireland.

For the Unionists, on the other hand, the idea of leaving out a certain number of Ulster counties forced them to change their plans. Carson and the other Unionist leaders now knew that they could not succeed in using Ulster to block Home Rule for the whole of Ireland. The best they could hope for was to keep a number of counties out of the plan. The question was, how many counties?

There are two Volunteer Forces in Ireland and two Flags.

This is THE FLAG of the ULSTER VOLUNTEER FORCE.

"Thee haughty tyrants ne'er shall tame;
All their attempts to bend thee down
Will but arouse thy generous flame,
And work their woe and thy renown.
'Rule, Britannia! Britannia rule the waves!
Britons never shall be slaves.'"

B A propaganda postcard. What do you think the other flag was? (See pages 48 and 54.)

The UVF

At the end of 1912 it seemed to the Unionists that they would have to step up their resistance if they were going to force Asquith to leave either all or part of Ulster out of the Home Rule Bill. So in January 1913 they formed the **Ulster Volunteer Force (UVF)**. The UVF needed 100,000 men and recruiting began immediately. As they hadn't very many weapons, the new recruits practised with dummy wooden rifles in Orange Halls all over Ulster.

To Redmond and the Nationalists the sight of men marching with dummy rifles was a bit of a joke. They warned Asquith that the Unionist threat of force was really only bluff. This helps to explain why the Liberal government took no action against the UVF even though the Unionists claimed that the UVF would be used against the government if it tried to force Home Rule on Ulster.

C

There will be a special parade of the Company on ... 17th inst., at 8 p.m. Full equipment to be worn by every man ... a fixed bayonet [will be supplied]. Commencing Saturday next at 6 p.m. every man is to attend Narrow Water shooting range and fire five rounds of the new Mauser rifle.

Orders issued by Commander of Warrenpoint Company, UVF, 14 July 1914

A group of Ulster Volunteers at Strabane, Co Tyrone

The nine counties of the Province of Ulster

Antrim	Donegal
Armagh	Down
Cavan	Fermanagh
Tyrone	Monaghan
Londonderry	

The Unionists were determined to make the UVF into a powerful force. To help with training their men, former officers of the British Army were brought in as full-time officers in the UVF. In July 1913 a retired English general, Sir George Richardson, arrived in Belfast to take command of the UVF. Under Richardson's direction, training weekends were held in each county on the estates of rich Unionist landowners. So it was soon clear that the UVF was becoming a well organised, highly trained and very determined force. The only thing missing was weapons, but Unionist leaders had already made secret plans to get weapons.

Questions

1 How can we tell from Source A that the forces of law and order did not object to UVF training?

2 What evidence is there in Source B that the UVF were proud of their British connection?

3 How do Sources C and D show that the UVF were taking seriously the threat to use force?

3.6 The Irish Volunteers

Near the end of 1913 there were signs that the Liberal government was beginning to have second thoughts about not giving special treatment to Ulster. While Asquith (the Prime Minister) continued to claim that no change would be made to the Home Rule plans for the whole of Ireland, other senior members of his government really believed that Ulster would have to be treated separately. Still, Asquith played down these difficulties in his talks with Redmond. The Irish Nationalist leader was happy to believe that the Liberal government would go ahead with Home Rule for the whole of Ireland.

But Nationalists in Ireland were not as hopeful as Redmond. They believed that the UVF was now so powerful that it was able to make the Liberal government change its ideas. What these Nationalists wanted was the same kind of force which could make sure that the Liberal government would not back down in the face of the Unionists. So, after seeing how the threat of force had helped the Unionist cause, these Nationalists formed the **Irish Volunteers** in November 1913. Their leader was a well known Dublin professor, **Eoin MacNeill**, who had earlier helped found the Gaelic League (see page 41). By the summer of 1914 the Irish Volunteers had well over 100,000 men, making it even bigger than the UVF.

A

Safeguard your rights and liberties (the few left you). Secure more.
Help your country to a place among the nations.
Give her a National Army to keep her there.
Get a gun and do your part.

Taken from a 1913 recruiting poster for the Irish Volunteers

Remember!

Redmond was the leader of the Irish Parliamentary Party which wanted Home Rule for the whole of Ireland.

B

A group of Volunteers from West Mayo

C

An Irish Volunteer gathering in Co Sligo

D

Unknown to the majority of Irish Volunteers themselves ... was the fact that they were secretly under the control of that small group of young men who ... had recently been [bringing back to life] the near defunct [dead] Irish Republican Brotherhood.

From *The Bold Fenian Men* by Robert Kee, 1972

1 What does Source C tell us about the level of support for the Irish Volunteers?

2 Which lines in Source A show that the Irish Volunteers would have been prepared to fight?

3 Why did members of the IRB join the Volunteer movement instead of openly reviving their own organisation?

uestions

Redmond and the Irish Volunteers

At first Redmond was shocked by the formation of the Irish Volunteers. Although the Volunteers still supported Home Rule, it was clear that many of them thought Redmond had become too moderate. More and more people joined the Irish Volunteers. Redmond knew he had to try to get control of it or else he might lose his own place as leader of the Nationalists.

Redmond was right to be worried by the sudden growth of the Irish Volunteers. The new force contained members of the old Fenian group. The Fenians were now called the Irish Republican Brotherhood (IRB) and many leading IRB figures had joined the Irish Volunteers on its formation. These men, who operated secretly within the Irish Volunteers, hoped to use the new force to gain something much more than Home Rule from the British. They wanted the complete separation of Ireland from Britain, and they were prepared to fight for it.

3.7 The Larne gun-running

A Unionist postcard

Members of the UVF loading their guns at Craigavon during the Curragh emergency, March 1914

B

All telegraph and phone wires to Larne were short-circuited that night. All telephone operators were "special" men.

At 11 pm a ship arrived in Belfast. Fifteen customs men were there; one asked "What's your cargo?"

The skipper replied "I am instructed to tell you it is coal."

Adapted from Captain F Hall's description of the gun-running, including the diversion staged at Belfast

Asquith was very alarmed that there were now two private armies in Ireland. Both the Ulster Volunteers and the Irish Volunteers wanted to bring weapons into Ireland. Asquith was afraid that this might lead to civil war. By the beginning of 1914 his main worry was the UVF.

The British government was afraid that the UVF might try to steal weapons from British army stores in Ulster. They thought about sending troops to Ulster from the main Army camp at the Curragh about twenty miles from Dublin. But even before orders to move to the North had been given, more than 50 officers told Army chiefs that they would resign rather than march into Ulster. This became known as the **Curragh Incident** and it put the UVF in a very strong position, because Carson and Craig (who led the UVF) now knew that Asquith could not risk using the British Army against them.

The UVF received further encouragement in April 1914 when a large shipment of arms was landed in the North. Back in January 1914 Carson and Craig had given their support to a plan to buy a huge cargo of weapons in Germany and bring them to Ulster. The man in charge of this gun-running plan was Fred Crawford.

D

A postcard issued in 1914 to celebrate the Larne gun-running

Many Nationalists had opposed Britain's actions against the Boers in the South African war, 1899-1902. In this postcard, a British soldier reminds Redmond of this fact.

E

No 18 P.C.

HAVE YOU FORGOTTEN?

BRITISH DISASTER IN SOUTH AFRICA CHEERED BY NATIONALIST MP's

SHALL BRITISH TROOPS BE USED AGAINST LOYAL ULSTER ?

On the night of the 24/25 April the arms finally arrived in Ulster on board the ***Clyde Valley***. This was a ship which Crawford had bought in Glasgow for £4,500.

Small numbers of weapons were landed at Bangor and Donaghadee, in County Down, but most of them were brought to Larne in Co Antrim. That night the UVF blocked off the town of Larne. They had a Motor Car Corps and these cars delivered the rifles all over Ulster very quickly. The police didn't try to stop the unloading and delivery of the weapons. To Nationalists it looked as if the police in Ulster were co-operating with the UVF.

In total nearly 25,000 rifles and three million rounds of ammunition had arrived. Now the Ulster Volunteers had the weapons to back up their threats of resisting Home Rule by force.

Questions

1 Would the UVF members, after the Curragh Incident, feel (a) angry, (b) surprised, or (c) encouraged? Explain your answer.

2 What evidence is there in the pictures that the Ulster Volunteers were prepared to use force?

3 How can you tell from this unit that the gun-running was well organised?

3.8 The Howth gun-running

After the Larne gun-running the Irish Volunteers were determined to organise their own gun-running. In fact, some of their leaders, including several IRB men, were already drawing up plans to bring in a big shipment of arms. Like the UVF, the Irish Volunteers bought the weapons in Germany and then sent them to Ireland on board a yacht owned by Erskine Childers, a well known Home Rule supporter. The yacht, the *Asgard*, arrived at Howth, Co Dublin, on 26 July 1914. A total of 1,500 rifles and 45,000 rounds of ammunition were landed at Howth harbour.

A

I saw at least a couple of hundred men running for all they were worth towards the pier ... while three or four hundred ran to the head of the pier ... Some of the men were in uniform, some had only badges, but all of them carried long oak life-preservers, and their officers carried revolvers in their hands. The majority of the men seemed to have come from Dublin. While they were running up the pier, the hatches of the yawl [small boat] were opened. Some of the men from the pier jumped down and handed up to their comrades rifles, wrapped in straw ... A very remarkable feature was that the whole affair was conducted almost in silence, very few orders being given.

The story of an eyewitness, reported in *The Irish Times*, 27 July 1914

B

A photograph taken at the time the guns were being unloaded at Howth, 26 July, 1914

C

Mrs Childers and Mary Spring-Rice on board the *Asgard* on its way to Ireland

The Bachelor's Walk Incident

But unlike Larne, the police at Howth tried to seize the arms that had been unloaded. To do this the police had asked for help and a small number of troops were ordered to the harbour. By this time a crowd had gathered and in the confusion the arms were slipped away in a fleet of taxis which had been waiting near the harbour. After failing to capture the arms the soldiers were ordered to march back to Dublin. On this three mile journey the soldiers were followed by some of the crowd who mocked them for their failure to seize the arms. When they reached **Bachelor's Walk**, which was a quay on the River Liffey, the soldiers suddenly opened fire. Three people were killed and 38 wounded. Nationalists were shocked and furious. They remembered that, only three months earlier, the police had stood by when a much larger shipment of arms had arrived in Larne. It was clear that the Irish Volunteers were being treated very differently to the UVF.

After the Howth gun-running there were two armed camps in Ireland. One in the South was determined to have Home Rule, while the other in the North was equally determined to stop Home Rule. Civil war now looked likely.

D

A deplorable affair occurred in Bachelor's Walk ... a force of King's Own Scottish Borderers marching back to barracks after intercepting National Volunteers who had been gun-running at Howth, were assailed by a mob, and retaliated by firing on the people.

The Irish Times, 27 July 1914

Questions

1 Who may have taken photographs B and C?

2 What does the presence of women suggest to you?

3 What evidence is there in Source C that the guns had come from Germany?

4 How does Source A confirm the scene pictured in Source B?

Activity

Divide into two groups to report the Bachelor's Walk incident. One group report from the point of view of a soldier, and the other from a Volunteer's viewpoint.

3.9   Ireland on the outbreak of war 1914

Ever since 1910 Redmond had stuck closely to the Liberals, believing that they would keep their promise to treat Ireland as a single nation and introduce Home Rule for the whole of Ireland. However, by March 1914 it was clear that the Liberals would not keep this bargain because they were ready with a new plan which they hoped would satisfy the Unionists. This was the **county option scheme**, and Redmond had no choice but to go along with it. County option meant that any county in Ireland could opt out of a Home Rule parliament for six years. This was to be decided by a vote taken in each county. The likely result of this scheme was that the four counties in North-East Ulster with a Protestant majority – Antrim, Down, Londonderry and Armagh – would opt out of Home Rule.

A

The Palace Conference is now a thing of the past. In a week, it has come and it has gone and in a sense the net result is nothing, for it has failed to bring forth a settlement that would avoid civil war.

Belfast Newsletter, 24 July 1914

Carson and the Unionists were against this idea. They had forced the government to leave four counties out of Home Rule, and they felt that if they dug in their heels they could get two more.

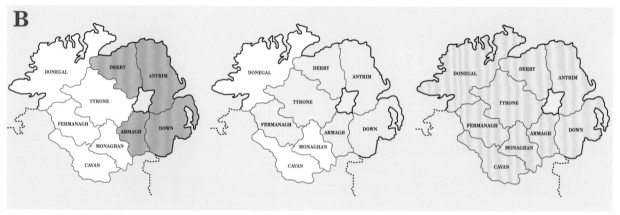

B

Ulster showing the three different options for the area to be left out of Home Rule

The Buckingham Palace Conference

Many people in England were waiting for civil war to break out in Ireland. King George V made one final try to get a compromise worked out. Representatives of the Liberals, Conservatives, IPP and Unionists took part in the **Buckingham Palace Conference** in July 1914. Although the party leaders talked about many ideas and examined lots of maps, they could not agree on the area of Ulster to be left out of Home Rule. Redmond would go no further than the four counties of Antrim, Down, Londonderry and Armagh, but Carson also wanted Tyrone and Fermanagh, even though both of these counties had small Nationalist majorities.

C

On 7 May 1915, a German submarine sank the passenger liner *Lusitania* off the coast of Ireland. Over 1,000 people were drowned.

The First World War

When the talks broke down, civil war was expected, but within a week a new crisis appeared which quickly pushed the Home Rule arguments into the background.

This was the **First World War**.

The war with Germany began in August 1914. Both Carson and Redmond wanted to show that their parties would give as much support as possible to Britain. Still, in September 1914 Asquith decided to tidy up the Home Rule mess. Unionists were angry when they learned that Home Rule was going to become law, though it was not to begin until the end of the war.

Asquith had also decided that the question of what to do about Ulster should be put off until the war was over. But the war was to strengthen the position of the Unionists and at the same time destroy Redmond and the IPP.

In class groups, prepare arguments in favour of three alternatives for Northern Ireland at that time —
4 county
6 county
9 county
You will find it helpful to look at the religious make-up of each county which is shown on page 77.

Activity

To **opt out** means to decide not to take part. To **compromise** with someone means neither of you gets everything you want, but you agree on some things in order to solve a problem.

1 Why do you think the King became involved?

2 Would you describe the mood or tone of the report in Source A as (a) hopeful (b) disappointed or (c) pleased? Explain your choice.

3 What is the message in Source C? How effective do you think it would be?

Questions

3.10   Irish Nationalists and the war

A

John Redmond at a passing out parade for Volunteers who have joined the British Army

B

Irishmen have two duties. One is to defend, at all costs, Ireland from any foreign invasion. Secondly, to prove how courageous Irishmen have always been in battle. I am encouraged to see around me so many men who would make good soldiers. I say to you – Go on drilling and get ready for whatever you are called to do in defence of right, freedom and religion in this war.

Adapted from John Redmond's speech to the Irish Volunteers at Woodenbridge, 20 September 1914

Redmond was determined to help the war effort. He thought that if Irish Nationalists fought for Britain, Ireland would be rewarded at the end of the war. But Redmond also believed that the war was a war for small nations. Germany had invaded Belgium, and like Ireland, Belgium was a small, Catholic country which Redmond thought Irish Nationalists should help. Six weeks after the war started Redmond made an important speech at **Woodenbridge**, Co Wicklow, in which he called on members of the Irish Volunteers to go to Belgium and France, where they would fight for the British Empire.

However, not all Irish Nationalists agreed with Redmond. While most of the Volunteers supported Redmond, about 10,000 broke away after the Woodenbridge speech and formed a new group under Eoin MacNeill. This group kept the name Irish Volunteers, while Redmond's much larger group became known as the **National Volunteers**. Many of these National Volunteers joined the British Army.

Redmond hoped that the two Irish Divisions of the British Army, the 10th and the 16th, which were mostly Nationalist and Catholic, would be joined together in a separate Irish Brigade. Although Asquith supported this, it did not happen, because the War Office, which organised things like this, didn't favour the Irish Nationalists as much as the Ulster Unionists. But this did not stop thousands of Irishmen joining the British Army.

1 How may the men of the 10th Irish Division have felt about the planning and organisation of the Gallipoli campaign?

2 Which aspects of the action at Messines would have (a) pleased and (b) not pleased the Irish soldiers?

3 Describe conditions in the trench shown in Source D.

Questions

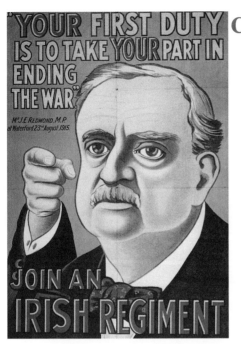

A recruitment poster showing John Redmond encouraging Irishmen to join the British Army

10th Irish Division troops at Gallipoli. These are soldiers of the Royal Irish Fusiliers. Note the special helmets used in the middle-east. In the foreground, soldiers are sleeping. Why has one soldier got his helmet on the end of his rifle?

Gallipoli

The first big action which the 10th Irish Division saw in the war was at Gallipoli, when it joined the famous Anzac forces in the landings in the Eastern Mediterranean. Here in August 1915 the Irish Division landed on the beaches at Gallipoli, where they were immediately attacked by the Turkish Army. They faced very harsh conditions. There wasn't enough water, the heat was terrible and the Turks were very tough enemies.

The Gallipoli campaign had been the idea of Winston Churchill (later Prime Minister but at this time he was just a government minister). From the start it was clear that it had been badly planned and was going to fail. Although they fought very bravely, the 10th Irish Division faced an impossible task and in just over a week 2,000 of its men were killed. In the end, the remains of the Irish Division and all the other parts of the British Army there had to leave.

Messines

Later in 1917 the 16th Division and the 36th Ulster Division (see unit 3.11) fought side by side at the Battle of Messines, which was in Belgium close to the French border. This time the Irish soldiers were successful. In June 1917, the 16th and 36th Divisions broke through German lines to score an important victory. This was followed by great celebrations, using large quantities of Irish whiskey, as former Irish Volunteers and Ulster Volunteers joined together to toast their victory. Surprisingly there weren't as many of their men killed at the Battle of Messines as expected. The 16th Division had 748 killed and wounded and the 36th had 700 killed and wounded.

Unfortunately the 16th Division lost one of their best known officers. Major Willie Redmond, a Home Rule MP and John Redmond's brother, was killed at Messines.

3.11 The Somme

This is a very famous painting, by JR Beadle, of the charge of the Ulster Division at the Battle of the Somme. The painting hangs in Belfast City Hall.

After the First World War began, Carson told the government that it could have trained members of the UVF to serve in the British Army. These UVF men were given their own separate division in the Army, the **36th Ulster Division**, which was to recruit 10,000 men. Recruiting in Ulster began immediately. Carson, Craig and the other Unionist leaders encouraged their supporters to join the new Ulster Division. They believed that if they helped Britain in her hour of need, the British would not force Home Rule on Ulster when the war was over. By April 1915 the Unionist newspaper, the *Belfast Newsletter*, was claiming that 35,000 men from Ulster had joined the British Army.

B

The organisation [UVF] has risen to a great occasion with ... enthusiasm ... bearing out to the full the frequent references of Sir Edward Carson to the loyalty of the Force and their readiness to do everything in their power to uphold [Britain] and to maintain the honour and prestige of the Empire.

From the *Belfast Newsletter*, 6 August 1914

C

Huge numbers of men on both sides were killed in the First World War. The armies on the Western Front were dug into trenches facing each other across what became known as No Man's Land. Neither side could get enough of an advantage to win. In the summer of 1916 the British decided to launch a very big infantry attack which they hoped would lead on to a final victory. The attack was to begin on 1 July 1916 close to the River Somme in northern France. The Ulster Division, which had only been sent to France in October 1915, was to be very important in the attack.

Activity

Find out how the Ulster Division's sacrifice at the Somme is remembered by loyalists in Ulster.

The **infantry** in an army are the foot soldiers. They don't ride horses or use any vehicles. The **Western Front** during the First World War was where the British and French faced the Germans.

The battle

From the moment it began, however, the attack turned out to be a disaster. About 20,000 British troops, including many Ulstermen, were killed on the first day of the battle, most of them in the first hour. The Ulster Division suffered very badly. Over 5,000 men were wounded, and of these at least 2,000 died. Although they suffered so badly, the Ulster troops fought very bravely, advancing further than any other division. So back in Ulster their families felt very proud as well as very sad.

Even though, as we saw in unit 3.10, Nationalist soldiers had fought very bravely and suffered great losses, the Unionist leaders always spoke of how the Ulster troops had fought and died for Britain in her hour of need. They were sure that the British would remember the great sacrifice at the Battle of the Somme when they came to think about the Ulster problem at the end of the war. So far as the Unionist leaders were concerned, forcing Ulster to accept any form of Home Rule was now out of the question.

Questions

1 Study Source A.

   (a) List the items carried by soldiers going to battle.

   (b) How does the picture show the dangers faced by infantry in the First World War?

2 What reasons, other than Carson's speeches, may have encouraged Ulstermen to join the British Army when war broke out?

3 If you were a relative or close friend of a soldier who died at the Somme, would the views expressed in Source C be the only type of feelings you would have had about his death? Explain your answer.

3.12 The Easter Rising - origins

A

Patrick Pearse as a young man

Most of the political leaders in Britain thought that the First World War would be over in a few months. Redmond thought this too. But by the beginning of 1916, it seemed that the war could drag on for years. This made more and more Irishmen turn against Redmond and his wartime support for Britain.

This opposition was led by the group of Irish Volunteers under Eoin MacNeill, which had broken away from Redmond at the start of the war and was still training and drilling as before (see page 62). They wanted to be trained and ready to make sure that the British gave them Home Rule at the end of the war. This breakaway group of Irish Volunteers also included a number of revolutionary nationalists or republicans, who were members of the secret IRB (Irish Republican Brotherhood). Soon after the start of the war some of these IRB men began to plan a rising or rebellion in which they hoped to use the Irish Volunteers to drive the British out of Ireland.

Patrick Pearse

The main person planning the rising was a Dublin school-master called **Patrick Pearse**. Pearse had also been an enthusiastic member of the Gaelic League. He started a school, St. Enda's, which had all of its subjects taught in Irish.

Others involved in the planning of the rising, such as **Thomas MacDonagh** and **Joseph Plunkett**, had also come into political life by being members of the Gaelic League. Indeed it was the coming together of the two types of nationalism, cultural (about national literature, games, music, and so on) and revolutionary (more violent), which

B

Irish Rebellion. May 1916.
Soldiers holding a Dublin Street.

British soldiers pose behind a barricade in a Dublin street, May 1916

produced a rising in 1916. At first, Pearse believed in more peaceful nationalism (see Unit 2.2), but now he was paying more attention to the old Fenian ideas and the sacrifices they had made for Ireland in the past. He also believed in the famous Fenian slogan: **"England's difficulty is Ireland's opportunity"**. This meant that the IRB would strike a blow for Irish freedom, while the British Army was busy fighting in the First World War.

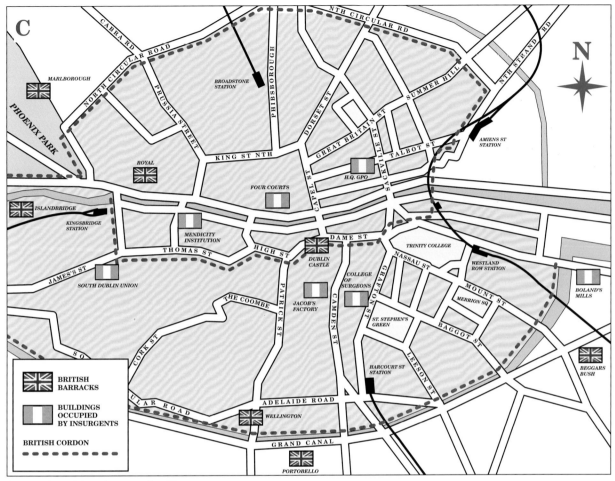

C

Central Dublin during the Rising

The date of the rising was fixed for **Easter 1916**. A man called **Roger Casement** had organised a big load of arms from Germany for the Irish Volunteers to use. However, these arms never reached Ireland and Casement was captured by the British. Without these arms, the Easter Rising was bound to fail, but Pearse and his IRB friends were determined to go ahead. They knew that they would be killed, but they thought that this blood sacrifice would stir up the people to demand freedom for Ireland.

Questions

1 Which household items can you identify in the barricade? (Source B)

2 What does this tell you about the preparation for trouble in that street?

3 Why do you think Pearse and his friends decided to go ahead with the rising, even after the capture of the arms?

4 Suggest reasons why Yeats ended his poem about Easter 1916 with the words "A terrible beauty is born". (Source D)

D

I write it out in a verse –
MacDonagh and MacBride
And Connolly and Pearse
Now and in time to be,
Wherever green is worn,
Are changed, changed utterly;
A terrible beauty is born.

From 'Easter 1916' by WB Yeats

3.13   The Easter Rising – results

An artist's impression of the scene inside the General Post Office, Dublin, just before the surrender, Easter, 1916. The man on the stretcher is James Connolly. Pearse stands beside him, bareheaded and holding a revolver.

The rising began on Easter Monday, 24 April 1916. About 1,500 Volunteers took part. Casement's capture had caused great confusion, because MacNeill called off the rising when he was told about it. In spite of the confusion, Pearse and his friends went on with their plans even though they must have known that the rising would be a hopeless failure.

Messengers were sent out around Dublin to organise as many men as possible for Easter Monday. The Volunteers' plan was to take over a number of important buildings in Dublin and hold out as long as they could. Their headquarters was the General Post Office (GPO) in O'Connell Street. Here the Volunteers ran up the flag of the Irish Republic over the building, and Pearse marched outside to read the Proclamation of the Republic. Many in the small crowd who listened could not believe what was happening.

The British had been taken by surprise, but because the Irish Volunteers just waited in the buildings until they were attacked, it was to be only a matter of time before the British defeated them.

Although they fought very bravely, their position was hopeless. On Saturday 29 April Pearse decided to surrender. The fighting had lasted less than a week and about 450 people were killed. Most people in Dublin were very angry with the Easter rebels and blamed them for the terrible damage which had been done to the city during the fighting.

Patrick Pearse posting the Proclamation of Independence outside the GPO. Ordinary life is shown going on in the background.

Executions

However, their anger at the rebels changed quickly when the British decided that those involved should be severely punished. After the rising the British Army chief in Dublin, Sir John Maxwell, took charge. He was told he could do what he liked with the rebel leaders. Following very quick trials fifteen of the leaders of the Easter Rising were executed by firing squad. The executions were spaced out between the 3 and 12 of May. Because

Dublin city centre in ruins after the rising. O'Connell Street is in the foreground and the River Liffey is on the right.

they were all carried out in secret, rumours quickly spread that more than 100 prisoners were to be executed. By the time the last leader, James Connolly, was executed most people were very sympathetic to the Easter rebels. In fact, the way Connolly was executed made many Irish people think of the leaders of the Easter Rising as heroes. Connolly had been badly wounded during the fighting. He was unable to stand up and so he had to be strapped to a chair to face the firing squad.

The British also rounded up nearly 3,500 suspects, but many of these had nothing whatsoever to do with the Easter Rising. The IRB had organised the rising, but the British did not know this. They blamed Sinn Fein.

The Irish voters turned against Redmond and the IPP after the rising. They gave their support to Sinn Fein.

D

We seem to have lost, we have not lost ... We have kept faith with the past and handed a tradition to the future ...

Patrick Pearse, speaking at his Court Martial in May 1916. A Court Martial is a court run by the Army.

1 Study Source A. What evidence is there in the picture that (a) many were dead or wounded and (b) fighting was still going on?

2 Describe the scene in O'Connell Street after the rising (Source C).

3 What do you think Pearse meant by the last sentence in Source D? (Clue: he always talked about the need for a "blood sacrifice".)

uestions

3.14 Markievicz, the Rebel Countess

A

Constance Markievicz –
born in 1868 as Constance
Gore-Booth

During the Easter Rising the Irish Volunteers were supported by a small force known as the **Irish Citizen Army** (ICA). James Connolly led the ICA. It had 200 members. It had been formed during the Dublin "lockout" in 1913. This lockout was a major strike in which the Dublin workers had to defend themselves against the police, while protesting against their employers.

After the strike, the ICA was reorganised by **Countess Markievicz**. She was born in 1868 and her first name was Constance. She belonged to a well known family from Co Sligo. In 1900 she married a Polish Count and this gave her the title, Countess. In 1909 she helped to set up a republican boy scouts movement, the **Fianna**. It was hoped that after their training some of these boys would go on to become members of the IRB.

Even though she had been brought up in the upper class of society, she became involved in working class politics by trying to help the Dublin poor. To begin with, she worked for equal rights for women and became a leading figure in the Irish suffragette movement, which wanted women to be given the vote. Before 1918 only men were allowed to vote.

But her main concern was for the poor living in Dublin. At that time the working class in Dublin lived in very bad slum dwellings. The Countess, who greatly admired James Connolly, was hard at work, trying to improve their conditions. This drew her towards socialism and the ICA. She was often to be found at Liberty Hall, the ICA's Dublin headquarters.

B

A photograph of Na Fianna Eireann (Irish National Boy Scouts) taken at their Fourth Annual Conference at the Mansion House, Dublin, 13th July 1913

C

Countess Markievicz led a Citizen Army contingent, wearing full uniform with a revolver in her belt.

A description of Markievicz at the funeral of the hunger-striker, Thomas Ashe, 30 September, 1917. From *The Green Flag*, Vol 3, by Robert Kee, 1972

D

You died for your country and
left me here
To weep – No! my eyes are dry
For the woman you found so
sweet and dear
Has a sterner destiny –
She will fight as she fought when
you were here;
For freedom I'll live and die.

A poem Markievicz wrote
about James Connolly after his
execution in 1916

E

She was to play a man's part in
and after 1916.

From *Ireland Since the Famine*
by FSL Lyons

Connolly decided that the ICA would take part in
the Easter Rising. Countess Markievicz supported
him. She was second-in-command of the group which
occupied Stephen's Green. After taking a careful look
at their position they moved to the building used by
the College of Surgeons on the west side of the Green.

The Countess was tall and good looking. She made
a striking figure in her uniform. She was also very
brave and displayed all the qualities of a good soldier
and leader during the week of the rising. After the
rebels surrendered, the Countess was put on trial with
the other leaders and she too was sentenced to death.
Much to her disgust the Countess was reprieved
because she was a woman!

Countess Markievicz (second from the right) under arrest
after the surrender by the rebels, Easter 1916

After her release she played a
leading role in Sinn Fein. In fact,
she became the first woman to be
elected to the British parliament when
she won a seat in the 1918 general
election, but like the other Sinn Fein
MPs she refused to take her seat at
Westminster.

After this she became Minister of
Labour in the Irish government. She
continued to be a politician up until
her death in 1927. She always took
the position of a staunch republican.

Questions

1 List all the interests which
Countess Markievicz had.

2 In what ways was she not typical
of an upper class Protestant
woman of that time?

3 What impression do Sources C,
D, E and F give of the sort of
woman she was?

4 Why do you think she was made
Minister of Labour in the Irish
government?

3.15 The Rise of Sinn Fein

A

A postcard issued by Sinn Fein following their success in the 1918 General Election

Sinn Fein was a more extreme nationalist group than the IPP. By calling the Easter Rising a Sinn Fein rebellion, even though Sinn Fein had nothing to do with the rising, the British gave Sinn Fein a great advantage. Sinn Fein could now defeat the IPP and demand a new settlement which would give Ireland much more independence than anything offered under Home Rule. In 1917, Sinn Fein won four by-elections. This showed how Irish voters were turning away from Redmond and the IPP and now supported Sinn Fein.

The most important of these by-elections took place in East Clare in July 1917. Here **Eamonn de Valera** won a great victory for Sinn Fein. De Valera, had been one of the leaders of the Easter Rising. He was lucky not to be executed but he was jailed. Soon after his release from jail he became President of Sinn Fein. In the East Clare by-election de Valera demanded full independence for Ireland. Like the other new Sinn Fein MPs, de Valera refused to take his seat in parliament. This idea was known as **abstention**, and it was very popular with Irish voters.

So after the Easter Rising, Sinn Fein was able to take advantage of the sympathy which many Irish people felt for those who had given their lives in 1916. They got more and more support during 1917. But it was yet another foolish mistake by the British which made sure of victory for Sinn Fein.

B

The bottom line of de Valera's policy was that he asked the voters of Clare to vote for a man who had fought for Ireland's independence; and who, if elected, would not take a seat in the British parliament. On polling day, 11th July 1917 ... he won the seat by a majority of more than two to one, 5,010 votes to 2,035.

From *De Valera — Long Fellow, Long Shadow* by Tim Pat Coogan, 1993

The conscription crisis

In March 1918 the Germans began a huge attack on the Western Front. The British soon found themselves short of men and they looked to Ireland to provide these extra troops. Ever since 1916 young men in Britain had to sign up to join the army. This was called **conscription**. In their desperate search for more men the British decided that conscription should be introduced in Ireland. This meant that Irishmen would be forced to join the British Army.

Remember!
All this time, from 1914 to 1918, the First World War was going on.

All Irish Nationalists, including Sinn Fein, the IPP and the Catholic Church, were angry at the British move and they were determined to stop it. In fact, opposition to conscription in Ireland was so great that the British soon decided to drop the idea. It was, of course, Sinn Fein which led the opposition, and when conscription was dropped the Irish people gave the credit to Sinn Fein. Indeed Sinn Fein had always tried to stop Irishmen joining the British Army, and though the IPP was also against conscription, many remembered how Redmond had encouraged men to join the army in 1914 and 1915.

The war ended in November 1918 and a general election was held in December. Because of the conscription crisis it was certain that Sinn Fein would win. It won a total of 73 seats. The IPP won only six. The Unionists, still a force in Ulster, won 26 seats. Many of the voters in 1918 had never voted before, and to these people Sinn Fein, with its energy and enthusiasm, seemed the right choice. John Redmond, the leader of the IPP, died early in 1918, but by then the IPP had very little influence left. In the 1918 general election it could not even find candidates to fight many of the seats. These seats went to Sinn Fein without a contest. The new Sinn Fein MPs, as they had promised, refused to go to Westminster. Instead they formed their own parliament in Dublin. It was called **Dail Eireann**, and its first meeting was held on **21 January 1919.**

C

Sinn Fein aims at securing the establishment of that Republic ... by making use of any and every means available to [make powerless] the power of England to hold Ireland [down] by military force or otherwise.

Extracts from the Sinn Fein election manifesto, 1918

Questions

1 Explain what is meant in Source A about the means which Sinn Fein would use to prevent the British government from taking away the people's rights.

2 Do you think people voted for de Valera more because of his part in the rising rather than his policy of abstention? Explain why you think so.

3 List the reasons why Irish Republicans would have found Sinn Fein's ideas attractive in 1918.

4 How can you tell from Source D that the man is not going willingly to war?

"The first Irish conscript" – an anti-conscription postcard

3.16 The War of Independence

A

This is a photograph of a train near Newry wrecked by the IRA in June 1921. Four soldiers were killed and also 80 cavalry horses used at the opening of the Northern Ireland Parliament, by King George V.

B

Michael Collins

C

Crown Casualties (ie police and army)

Jan. - Sept. 1920
125 killed 235 wounded

Sept. 1920 - 11th July 1921
400 killed 700 wounded

Civilian Casualties (including the IRA)

Jan. - July 1921
707 killed 756 wounded
Of the 707 killed, over 100 were shot by the IRA as "spies"

Quoted in *The Green Flag* by Robert Kee, 1972

During the general election campaign in 1918, Sinn Fein had said that it would go to the **Peace Conference** to put Ireland's case for independence. Many other small nations were going to the Peace Conference with the same aim. Irish voters liked this idea, but when the Peace Conference met in Paris at the beginning of 1919 the Sinn Fein representatives were ignored by the American and European leaders. This left Sinn Fein unsure about what its next move should be.

In the meantime the Irish Volunteers took action. On 21 January 1919, the same day as the first meeting of Dail Eireann, a small band of Volunteers killed two members of the Royal Irish Constabulary (RIC) who were taking a load of explosives to a quarry. This happened at Soloheadbeg in Co Tipperary, and it marked the beginning of the **War of Independence**. Other attacks followed and by the end of 1919 a total of 14 policemen and soldiers had been killed.

These attacks shocked the people, because the RIC men were often well known in the local area and their killings were condemned by the Catholic Church. Yet, once again, the British reaction to these attacks soon changed people's views. By 1920 the Volunteers, or **Irish Republican Army** (IRA) as they were now known, were engaged in a guerilla war campaign in different areas of the country, mainly in Cork and Tipperary.

The Black and Tans

The British would not accept that the IRA was fighting a real war, and so instead of sending extra troops to Ireland the British decided to make the RIC stronger. To do this they signed up a number of ex-soldiers and sent them across to Ireland. As the new force wore a mixture of police and military uniforms, they were nicknamed the **Black and Tans**. These Black and Tans lacked training and discipline. If they were attacked, they often took revenge on ordinary people living in the area. These reprisals, as the revenge attacks were called, quickly put local people on the IRA's side.

A **guerilla** war is a war which is fought by small bands of soldiers, usually without uniform. They use 'hit and run' tactics to attack when the opportunity arises.

D

Dublin yesterday was the scene of an unprecedented outbreak of organised crime, resulting in the murders of twelve Army officers associated with the bringing to justice of Sinn Fein gunmen ... Later in the day, forces of the crown, proceeding to the venue of a Gaelic football match to [make] arrests, were fired on by a Sinn Fein "picket". The fire was returned and 10 people were killed and over 50 wounded. After the fighting, between 30 and 50 revolvers were found by the troops and police inside the football grounds.

Belfast Newsletter, 22 November 1920

The IRA then stepped up its attacks. Its campaign was masterminded by a young man from Co Cork, **Michael Collins**. In Dublin Collins was head of a secret group called the Squad which killed 11 suspected British agents on the morning of 21 November 1920. That Sunday afternoon British forces fired on a crowd at a gaelic football match in Croke Park, killing 12 people and wounding 60 others. The day was called Bloody Sunday. Ten days later the IRA killed 17 British troops in an ambush in Co Cork.

The fighting was now so bad that the British had to think again about using the Black and Tans. At the same time Collins knew that no matter how hard the IRA fought, it could not drive the British out of Ireland. So both sides now agreed to end the war and a truce was signed between Sinn Fein and the British government in July 1921. The War of Independence was over, but the two sides now had to work out a treaty.

It was December 1921 before Sinn Fein and the British government signed the **Anglo-Irish Treaty**. Although the Treaty did not give the South full independence, Sinn Fein had won much more freedom than Home Rule could have given. The British government hoped that the Treaty had finally settled the Irish Question.

Questions

1 Why do you think the train in Source A was ambushed?

2 Would the figures in Source C suggest that the fighting was worse in 1920 or 1921? Explain your answer.

3 Pick out sentences from Source D which give the impression

   (a) that the army officers who were shot were seen by the IRA to be "legitimate" targets;

   (b) that the police action in Croke Park was taken in self defence;

   (c) that the crowds at Croke Park were prepared for trouble.

4 How do you think the fact that this report came from a Unionist paper affects its reliability?

3.17 Partition

While the War of Independence was being fought, the British government returned to the problem of Ulster. The Prime Minister, who was now **David Lloyd George**, had set up a committee to work out a solution to the Ulster problem. The committee's main proposal was **partition**. This introduced a border which divided Ireland into two parts, Northern Ireland and what became known as the Irish Free State. The big question for the committee to sort out was how many counties should be in Northern Ireland. The members of the committee thought that it should include the nine counties of Ulster, but at the last moment the government reduced the number of counties from nine to six. This was what the Ulster Unionist leaders wanted. They knew that a nine county area, which included Cavan, Monaghan and Donegal, would mean that they were only just a majority. A six county area would give the Unionists a safe majority.

Partition was brought into force by the **Government of Ireland Act** which became law in 1920. It also made the arrangements for the new Northern Ireland Parliament, and elections for it were held in May 1921. Unionists surprised themselves by winning 40 of the 52 seats, an even bigger majority than they expected. The other 12 seats were shared equally between the IPP and Sinn Fein who had made a deal before voting took place. The new parliament met in Belfast City Hall. It was opened by the King in June 1921.

A

... it was evident that any decision of the [Boundary] Commission would be dominated by the voice of the chairman representing the British government.

From the unpublished memoirs of Eoin MacNeill, quoted in *The Scholar Revolutionary*

B

Deannáct na Féile Pádraig

When thinking of Ireland on St. Patrick's Day remember—

Slemish

Armagh

Downpatrick

✠ That the Irish nation has been partitioned by Britain against the will of the overwhelming majority of the people ;

✠ That the essence of democratic rule is contained in the right of a people to determine its own affairs without outside interference ;

✠ That St. Patrick's See at Armagh, his grave at Downpatrick and the scenes of his boyhood on Slemish are cut off from the body of Ireland and are in the area occupied by British troops in a flagrant denial of all democratic rights.

On this St. Patrick's Day pledge yourself to help to undo the dismemberment of St. Patrick's Island

This St Patrick's Day card was issued about 1922, showing the border of the new Northern Ireland.

C

(i) There would be separate Parliaments for Southern and Northern Ireland.

(ii) Northern Ireland would consist of the counties of Antrim, Armagh, Down, Derry, Fermanagh and Tyrone and the parliamentary boroughs of Belfast and Derry.

(iii) A Council of Ireland will comprise of a President, appointed by the King, and forty members chosen equally by the two Houses of Parliament.

(iv) Southern parliament to have 128 members; Northern parliament to have 52 members.

(v) Forty-two Irish members in the House of Commons of the United Kingdom.

(vi) The Home Rule Act of 1914 to be repealed.

Adapted from the terms of the 1920 Government of Ireland Act

It was during the Anglo-Irish Treaty negotiations towards the end of 1921 that Sinn Fein heard about the British view of partition. The British did not like it and did not think that it would last. They saw partition as a temporary measure, and this is why the Government of Ireland Act arranged for a Council of Ireland to be set up. Its aim was to prepare the way for the unification of Ireland which most British politicians expected. At the same time the Anglo-Irish Treaty promised Sinn Fein that a **Boundary Commission** would be set up to suggest changes to the new border. The Unionist leaders were afraid that this could lead to some border areas being handed over to the Irish Free State. The areas in question all had large Nationalist majorities. Parts of South Down and South Armagh, as well as most of Tyrone and Fermanagh, could be handed over in such an arrangement.

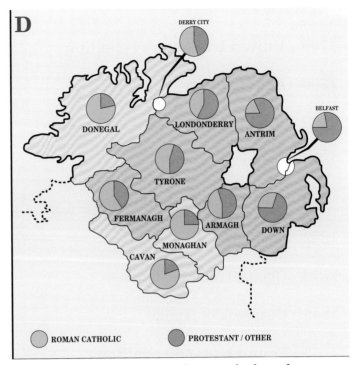

The nine counties of Ulster showing the boundary of Northern Ireland. The circles show how many Protestants and Catholics were in each county, according to a census taken in 1911.

Of course, partition was a compromise. The British had been unable to come up with any other plan which both Unionists and Nationalists could accept. Yet while Nationalists hoped that partition would not last, Unionists were determined to make it permanent.

Partition also created new problems. The Irish Free State and Northern Ireland were not going to be friendly neighbours and partition had left a large number of Nationalists in Northern Ireland. They made up one third of the population and from the start these Northern Nationalists were desperate for the border to be removed so that Ireland could once again be a united country.

Activity

In groups, prepare speeches for and against the terms of the Government of Ireland Act. Can you think of a better solution to the Irish problem?

Questions

1 What evidence is there in Source A that Irish Nationalists were not hopeful about the outcome of the Boundary Commission?

2 Why are Downpatrick, Slemish and Armagh marked on the postcard (Source B) ?

3 How would the following react to the terms of the Government of Ireland Act: Ulster Unionists; moderate (non-violent) Nationalists; Irish Republicans?

4 Which groups in Ulster would not have been pleased with the decision to have the six county option?

5 Which groups in Ireland may have disapproved of having a President of the Council of Ireland appointed by the King?

6 Which arguments might people in the South have put forward against equal representation in the Council of Ireland? (Clue - how many counties in each part of Ireland?)

Chronology

1798 **United Irishmen's rebellion**

1800 **Act of Union**

1803 **Robert Emmet's rebellion**

1813 Irish Constabulary formed

1829 **Catholic Emancipation**

1842 Young Ireland formed

1843 Clontarf Meeting banned

1845 Outbreak of famine

1848 **Young Ireland rebellion**

1849 Queen Victoria visited Ireland

1850 End of the famine

1858 Fenian movement (IRB) formed
Harland and Wolff founded

1867 **Fenian Rising**

1870 Home Rule Movement founded

1875 Parnell became an MP

1879 **Land League founded**
Land War began
Death of Isaac Butt

1880 Parnell leader of Home Rule Party
Boycotting began

1881 **Gladstone's Land Act**

1882 Parnell imprisoned
Land War ended

1884 **Gaelic Athletic Association founded**

1886 **First Home Rule Bill**

1890 O'Shea divorce scandal

1891 Split in Home Rule Party
Death of Parnell
Irish Unionist Alliance formed

1892 Ulster Unionist Convention

1893 **Second Home Rule Bill**
Gaelic League founded

1894 Irish Agricultural Organisation Society formed

1899 Department of Agriculture set up

1900 John Redmond reunited the IPP

1903 **Wyndham Land Act**

1905 **Sinn Fein founded**

1909 Fianna (boys movement) formed

1911 Parliament Act

1912 Sinking of the *Titanic* (April)
Third Home Rule Bill (April)
Ulster Covenant (Sept)

1913	Ulster Volunteer Force formed (Jan) Irish Volunteer Force formed (Nov) Irish Citizen Army formed (Nov)
1914	Curragh Incident (March) **Larne gun-running (April)** Buckingham Palace Conference(July) **Howth gun-running (July)** Outbreak of war (Aug) Split in Irish Volunteers (Sept)
1915	Gallipoli campaign
1916	**Easter Rising (April)** Battle of the Somme (July)
1917	Battle of Messines Ridge Sinn Fein by election victories
1918	Conscription Crisis End of First World War General Election (Dec)
1919	**First meeting of Dail Eireann** Start of War of Independence
1920	Black and Tans formed **Government of Ireland Act**
1921	Partition of Ireland (June) End of War of Independence (July) **Anglo-Irish Treaty (Dec)**
1922	Irish Free State formed (Jan)

The Conservative Party

Conservatives believed in traditions that were important to the English people — like the House of Lords, the Monarchy and the Church of England. They did not like a lot of change and reform. They wanted England to have a large empire, and were against Ireland becoming independent. They supported the Union and, after 1885, backed the Irish Unionists.

The Liberal Party

Liberals believed in freedom (liberty) and were keen to see change and reform. They did not want the Monarchy to have much power. They were supported in England by people who were not Church of England. They stood up for the rights of Ireland, Scotland and Wales. After 1885 Liberals supported Irish Home Rule. Most Irish people living in England voted Liberal.

The Home Rule Party

This party wanted Ireland to have its own parliament in Dublin, but accepted that Ireland would remain in the United Kingdom. After 1885 they were allied to the Liberals. Most party supporters were Catholic.

The Unionist Party

Unionists were against Home Rule and did not want a parliament in Dublin. Most Unionists were Protestant and supported the Conservatives.

Index

Asquith, Herbert   44, 52–54, 61

Belfast   4–5, 20–25, 34–35
Black and Tans   75
Butt, Isaac   30, 36

Carson, Sir Edward   46, 47, 49, 51, 52, 56, 60, 61, 64
Collins, Michael   75
Connolly, James   68–71
Craig, Sir James   46, 47, 50, 56
Curragh Incident   56

Davitt, Michael   16
de Valera, Eamon   72

Easter Rising   66–69, 72
Elections   30 (1874) 32, 37 (1885), 44 (1910), 71, 73 (1918), 76 (1921)
Emigration   13–15
Emmet, Robert   28–29

Famine   8–16
Fenian Brotherhood   29
First World War   61–65

Gaelic Athletic Association 40
Gaelic League   41, 54, 66
Gallipoli   63
Gladstone, W. E.   17, 31, 34, 35, 37, 38
Government of Ireland Act   76
Griffith, Arthur   43

Harland and Wolff   22–24
Home Rule Bills   31, 34, 37 (1886); 31, 35 (1893); 45, 47, 61 (1912)
Home Rule Party (IPP) 16, 30, 37, 39, 44, 60, 72, 73
Howth gun-running   58–59

Hyde, Douglas   41

Irish Republican Brotherhood   29, 43, 55, 66, 69
Irish Volunteers   54–55, 58–59, 62, 67, 68, 74

Land Acts   18 (1881), 19, 43 (1903)
Land League   16, 17, 36, 37
Larne gun-running   56–57
Law, Andrew Bonar   44, 45, 47
Linen industry   20–21

MacNeill, Eoin   41, 54, 66, 68
Markievicz, Countess   70–71

National Volunteers   62–63

O'Connell, Daniel   30
O'Shea, Katherine   38–39

Parnell, Charles Stuart   16, 36–39
Partition   52, 60, 76–77
Pearse, Patrick   66–68
Population   4, 6, 8, 14, 22

Redmond, John   44, 49, 53–55, 57, 60–63

Shipbuilding   23–25
Sinn Fein   43, 69, 72–73, 76–77
Somme, Battle of   64–65

Tenant farmers   6–7, 14, 16, 18
Titanic   22, 25
Tone, Wolfe   28
Treaty, Anglo-Irish   75

Ulster Covenant   50–51
Ulster Volunteers   52-53, 56–57, 63–64
Union, Act of   4, 24–26, 30
United Irishmen   28

Young Ireland   29